Cambridge Elements ☰

Elements in Eighteenth-Century Connections
edited by
Eve Tavor Bannet
University of Oklahoma
Rebecca Bullard
University of Reading

EMPIRICAL KNOWLEDGE IN THE EIGHTEENTH-CENTURY NOVEL

Beyond Realism

Aaron R. Hanlon
Colby College

CAMBRIDGE
UNIVERSITY PRESS

CAMBRIDGE
UNIVERSITY PRESS

Shaftesbury Road, Cambridge CB2 8EA, United Kingdom

One Liberty Plaza, 20th Floor, New York, NY 10006, USA

477 Williamstown Road, Port Melbourne, VIC 3207, Australia

314–321, 3rd Floor, Plot 3, Splendor Forum, Jasola District Centre,
New Delhi – 110025, India

103 Penang Road, #05–06/07, Visioncrest Commercial, Singapore 238467

Cambridge University Press is part of Cambridge University Press & Assessment,
a department of the University of Cambridge.

We share the University's mission to contribute to society through the pursuit of
education, learning and research at the highest international levels of excellence.

www.cambridge.org
Information on this title: www.cambridge.org/9781108791649

DOI: 10.1017/9781108866378

First published 2022

A catalogue record for this publication is available from the British Library.

ISBN 978-1-108-79164-9 Paperback
ISSN 2632-5578 (online)
ISSN 2632-556X (print)

Empirical Knowledge in the Eighteenth-Century Novel

Beyond Realism

Elements in Eighteenth-Century Connections

DOI: 10.1017/9781108866378
First published online: November 2022

Aaron R. Hanlon
Colby College
Author for correspondence: Aaron R. Hanlon, arhanlon@colby.edu

Abstract: This Element examines the eighteenth-century novel's contributions to empirical knowledge. Realism has been the conventional framework for treating this subject within literary studies. This Element identifies the limitations of the realism framework for addressing the question of knowledge in the eighteenth-century novel. Moving beyond the familiar focus in the study of novelistic realism on problems of perception and representation, this Element focuses instead on how the eighteenth-century novel staged problems of inductive reasoning. It argues that we should understand the novel's contributions to empirical knowledge primarily in terms of what the novel offered as training ground for methods of reasoning, rather than what it offered in terms of formal innovations for representing knowledge. We learn from such a shift that the eighteenth-century novel was not a failed experiment in realism, or in representing things as they are, but a valuable system for reasoning and thought experiment.

Keywords: novel, Enlightenment, epistemology, data, knowledge

Isbns: 9781108791649 (PB), 9781108866378 (OC)
Issns: 2632-5578 (online), 2632-556X (print)

Contents

Introduction

This Element examines the eighteenth-century British novel's contributions to empirical knowledge, or how we move from observations to generalizations. It's a deceptive topic because it slips easily between literary history and philosophy. It's also a familiar topic in the study of the novel, particularly of novelistic realism. Since Ian Watt's influential and enduring *The Rise of the Novel*, scholars of literature have addressed questions of knowledge in the eighteenth-century novel largely through the rubric of what Watt calls "formal realism," which is not "the kind of life" the novel presents, but "the way it presents it" (Watt, 2001, p. 11). Not everyone agrees with Watt's central thesis that "the novel raises more sharply than any other literary form" "the problem of correspondence between the literary work and the reality which it imitates," but even Watt's critics tend to understand the relationship between the novel and empirical knowledge as a matter of the epistemic problem of correspondence plus the formal problem of representation (Watt, 2001, p. 11). The central claim of this Element is that the eighteenth-century novel made its most dynamic and enduring contributions to empirical knowledge not through formal strategies of representation, but as a training ground for inductive reasoning.

Modern disciplinary divisions have shaped our understanding of the eighteenth-century British novel's impact on empirical knowledge, often in limiting ways. Philosophers address relationships between truth and fiction or aesthetics and propositional knowledge, often drawing examples from fiction, but not typically from eighteenth-century fiction. Philosophy of fiction is part of the broader subfield of aesthetics, and philosophers of fiction tend to agree with literature scholars that eighteenth-century literature is not aesthetically exemplary of what today we consider literature (this is a euphemistic way of saying that even literature scholars tend to turn up their noses at eighteenth-century fiction, while philosophers draw the bulk of their examples from the more celebrated literary traditions: classical Greek and Roman, nineteenth-century British, US, and Russian literatures, and of course Shakespeare). Meanwhile, historians of philosophy chart developments in eighteenth-century theories of knowledge in the work of figures canonized as philosophers – Francis Bacon, Rene Descartes, John Locke, David Hume, and the like – without accounting for the philosophical contributions of other genres of writing in the period, a period that predates the division of writing into "literature" and "philosophy." One unfortunate side effect of the disciplinary division between literary studies (concerned more with form and representation than with knowledge) and history of philosophy (concerned with "philosophy" as a retroactively identified genre that largely excludes novelistic fiction when not written by authors since canonized as "philosophers") is that the philosophical contributions of women, working primarily in the medium of novelistic fiction, go under-recognized in the history of Enlightenment philosophy (I explain more about this later).

As a consequence of the structural gap between literary studies and philosophy, literature scholars have largely confined ourselves to addressing the relationship between fiction and knowledge through the back door of novelistic realism, reducing epistemic matters to matters of form and representation. The purpose of this Element is to account for the structural gap between literary history and philosophy that leads scholars to understand the question of empirical knowledge in the eighteenth-century novel as a question of realism, where realism equals the problem of correspondence plus the problem of representation. What's missing from this equation hides in plain sight: reasoning, specifically systems of inference. In other words, what's missing from the abundance of writing on empirical knowledge in the eighteenth-century novel is how the novel illustrates and embodies systems of thought, or what happens between observation or representation and justified true belief.

Accordingly, to adopt realism as the primary framework for this topic would be to limit this study in precisely the ways I aim to correct. What Karin Kukkonen calls "the curse of realism" – the retroactive imposition of the aesthetic standards of nineteenth-century novels on prior novels, such that eighteenth-century novels come to look like failed versions of latter realisms to which they never aspired – is one more reason to move away from realism as a framework for understanding the eighteenth-century novel's contributions to empirical knowledge (Kukkonen, 2019, pp. 9–11). For Kukkonen, Lisa Zunshine, and other scholars working in the field of cognitive literary studies, challenging traditional notions of novelistic realism paved the way for readings of novels that bring evolutionary and cognitive science to bear on novelistic moments of perception. However, this Element is not a study in cognitive poetics, but a study in the philosophy of novelistic fiction. Answering the question of how or whether novelistic strategies of representation achieve a plausible or probable degree of correspondence with the real is important, but it's not enough for knowledge. Empirical systems entail systems of reasoning from observations *or* representations. In an empirical system, knowledge does not follow deductively from observation; empiricism needs induction, a system for drawing general conclusions from specific observations. The eighteenth-century British novel made its most under-appreciated and important contributions to empirical knowledge not through unique strategies for representing the real, but through portrayals of reasoning and thought experiment.

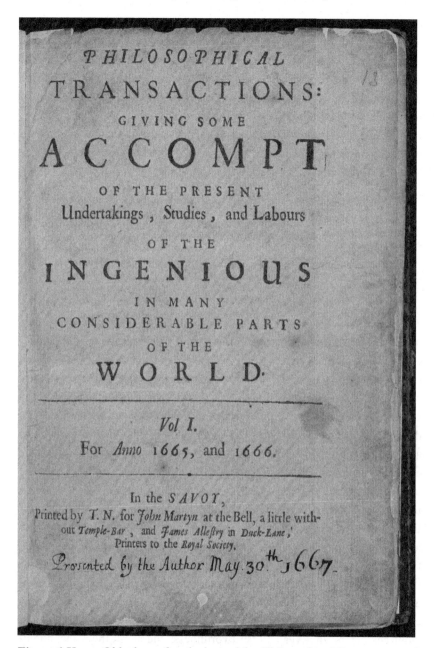

Figure 1 Henry Oldenburg, frontispiece of the *Philosophical Transactions of the Royal Society*, 1666 (licensed under **CC-BY-4.0**)

Like the study of novelistic realism, the study of seventeenth- and eighteenth-century empiricism, particularly of the Baconian kind and its afterlife in Royal Society writing and experimental practice, has heaped much of the pressure of justifying knowledge claims on the moment of observation or experience and the objectivity of the observer. However, the widely observed fact that Royal Society scientific atlases rhetorically stressed the clarity and fidelity of pictures over words while relying on verbal descriptions and explanations is evidence that even natural philosophers who were hyper-focused on the fidelity of representation understood the necessity of inference and explanation. Knowledge never simply arrived in the picture, nor did pictures capture the intellection that takes place during and after a sensory experience. As Alex Wragge-Morley writes,

> "naturalists had powerful philosophical motivations for accompanying pictures with verbal descriptions. They did not resort to descriptions simply because their desire to use pictures was thwarted by the high cost of having engraved plates made. They were also motivated by a conception of experience that, in most instances, made the production of pictorial representations that truly resembled their objects impossible"
>
> (Wragge-Morley, 2020, pp. 124–125).

The study of novelistic realism has put a comparable amount of pressure on novelistic representation as the cornerstone of the novel's epistemic success or failure. This makes sense because representation – well beyond questions of epistemology – has always been a central interest in literary studies, at least as central as objectivity has been to the history of the empirical sciences. But representation and objectivity, in their respective disciplinary domains, can carry our understanding of empirical knowledge and the novel only so far. The study of empirical knowledge in the eighteenth-century British novel is due for a revision akin to the one undertaken in the history of early modern natural philosophy. Whereas historians of science have taken greater account of the affective and aesthetic dimensions of early modern ways of knowing, the study of empirical knowledge in the eighteenth-century novel requires an account of novelistic portrayals of reasoning as necessary for empirical knowledge. Novels illustrated not only moments of apprehension or sensory experience, but also what happens after, including how characters process sensory experiences and subsequently move to conclusions about their worlds, about other characters' motives and trustworthiness, and about their own cognitive limitations and biases.

I have suggested that the study of the eighteenth-century novel's contributions to empirical knowledge has been constrained by the rubric of formal realism, even when scholars disagree with Watt's definition of formal realism or his claims about its influence or generic specificity (that is, whether formal

Figure 2 Frontispiece to *The History of the Royal Society of London* (1702 edition) featuring Francis Bacon on the right (Evelyn, 1667)

realism is a property belonging only or especially to the novel genre). Here I'll explain a bit more what I mean by that. Consider two influential, oppositional lines of thought about the eighteenth-century novel and empirical knowledge.

The first is in the vein of Watt's thesis. John Bender observes that eighteenth-century novels "share a way of representing the world and the kind of verisimilitude that Steven Shapin and Simon Schaffer in *Leviathan and the Air-Pump* call 'virtual witnessing' . . . the rhetorical and visual apparatus for communicating scientific experiments to the public and convincing that public of their authenticity" (Bender, 1998, p. 8). For Bender, through verisimilar representations, "fictions, be they hypotheses or novels, yield a provisional reality, an 'as if', that possesses an explanatory power lacking in ordinary experience." It's this fictive, provisional reality from which, as Bender argues, science required separation, or the ability to differentiate between stylistically or representationally similar statements in fiction and in experimental natural philosophy. I'll return to the specifics of Bender's broader argument, but for now I only point out that for Bender, as for Watt, verisimilar "generic traits," produced amid a heightened Enlightenment cultural desire to certify or validate knowledge, mark the novel's special relationship to the development of empirical knowledge (Bender, 1998, p. 9).

The second line of thought is Helen Thompson's critique both of Steven Shapin and Simon Schaffer's claims about the importance of virtual witnessing to Royal Society experimental natural philosophy and of "scholars from Bruno Latour to John Bender," who affirm "the constitutive exclusion of imperceptible causality from the new science" (Thompson, 2016, p. 12). Thompson challenges the "ultimate realist premise" of the first line of thinking:

> The novel, I argue, invokes things that cannot be sensed, things whose power to produce sensation is not mimetically transmitted by sensation itself . . . my account is neither dualist nor Cartesian. Indeed, although *Rise of the Novel* precedes Shapin and Schaffer's exposition of experimental science, a key feature of Watt's realism anticipates their claim for the literal visibility of empirical fact: the "one-to-one correspondence" of referent to reality bars insensible causes from the novel as well as from experiment. My book disputes this "ultimate realist premise" by challenging the dualist presumption that segregates references to mind from references to body. Instead, I argue, eighteenth-century novels make explicit the *production* of sensational understanding as the reader's encounter with forms and powers that enable empirical knowledge. (Thompson, 2016, p. 17)

In conceiving of the novel as a means of representing the qualitative experience of sense perception and of the imperceptible – as opposed to mimetic or verisimilar representation of the real – Thompson demonstrates the shortcomings of the realist theses of Watt and Bender, but *maintains their focus on the novel's formal or representational engagement with the moment of apprehension or perception*, or as Thompson puts it, "the forms, relations, and powers through which empirical apprehension of reality happens" (Thompson, 2016, p. 11). "The realism that empirical knowledge bequeaths literary history," writes Thompson, "is not mimetic reflection of objects in the world. This realism entails the figures, forms, and experiences through which novels think the contingently produced event of qualitative understanding" (Thompson, 2016, p. 3).

Between the Watt-Bender thesis and the Thompson thesis, we have generative disagreement over the novel's relationship to empirical knowledge. This disagreement both draws on and gives rise to numerous additional accounts of novelistic representation and empirical knowledge in the eighteenth century. But the common focus of even oppositional studies of the topic is the integrity of this formula: the problem of correspondence (verisimilitude) plus the problem of representation (figures, forms). Jonathan Kramnick neatly articulates this focus in a meditation on "Empiricism, Cognitive Science, and the Novel": "To have a mental state is to be in view of a representation, a picture of something one experiences or a series of pictures one puts together, and to be in view of a representation is to be in some relation of greater or lesser accuracy to a world that is being depicted" (Kramnick, 2007, p. 265). Thompson and Natania Meeker, in their introduction to the journal issue that frames Kramnick's article among others, note that "in the eighteenth century, fiction and philosophy substantially intervene in shaping acts of perception, thus constituting and reconstituting experience as materiality" (Thompson and Meeker, 2007, p. 185). I have suggested such a focus makes sense in light of the disciplinary interest of literary studies in matters of representation, but Jonathan Lamb explains another reason for such a focus: the line of thought in Locke, Boyle, Hobbes, and others that takes truth as "a credible representation of what our limited senses allow us to experience" (Lamb, 2007, p. 196). Each of these examples reflects a common way of understanding empirical knowledge in the strict sense of the perceptual and experiential, as a function of the moment of apprehension or sensation and the extent to which it grants us access to the real. This is what scholars typically pick up on in novelistic representation, whether framed as verisimilar (Watt-Bender) or experiential (Thompson-Meeker).

My aim in this Element is not to contest wholesale the vast amount of scholarly work on perception and representation as focal points for explaining the novel's contributions to empirical knowledge. Rather, I claim a negative externality of the momentum generated by interest in perception and representation is that novelistic portrayals of and inducements to processes of reasoning drop out of the equation. This is a problem, because seventeenth- and eighteenth-century empiricists well understood that, representation aside, sense data may be the best basis we have for drawing conclusions, but does not constitute reliable knowledge in its own right. This is precisely why the forms of Baconian inductive empiricism that would become the dominant theory of knowledge in Britain during the eighteenth century took experiments and experimental technologies as means of countervailing the psychological and cognitive limits – or features, as the case may be – of the human mind.

Accordingly, this Element focuses on how eighteenth-century novels treat reasoning processes. Of course this entails accounts of perception and representation, but not as epistemic ends so much as starting points for what the novel teaches us about methods of inference and justification. As I will show, eighteenth-century writers were adept either at isolating the problems of correspondence and perception to foreground methods of reasoning, or putting so much pressure on the reliability of empirical observation that illustrations of reasoning become the only way out of the forest. In such ways, the novel both evinced and furthered understandings of empirical knowledge projects in the period.

Induction is the primary form of reasoning I address in this Element. I mean induction broadly construed as synthetic reasoning from gathered observations, and for which premises are evidence-based but do not guarantee the truth of the conclusion. The problem of induction concerns, as Ian Hacking puts it, whether "any number of observed instances, short of a complete survey, ever make it reasonable to believe a generalization" (Hacking, 1975, p. 176). The nature, boundaries, and reliability of inductive inference are long-contested, seemingly intractable questions in philosophy, and as such beyond the scope of this study. But that's also why it's worth turning to fiction, and to the eighteenth-century novel in particular, for illustrations of rationales and thought processes that rely on various kinds of inductive leaps. If everyday life – portrayals of which justified theories of the novel as a new and distinct genre for Henry Fielding, Frances Burney, and others – were always or even mostly amenable to deductive reasoning as a practical tool for validating everyday conclusions, then we might not have cause to gather novelistic data of inductive thinking. Alas, as Hume recognized, inductive thinking is both fundamentally flawed and broadly necessary.

Bender offers perhaps the most direct treatment of the role of induction in the novel's contributions to empirical knowledge. He correctly identifies the eighteenth-century British novel as "part of a cultural system that worked to validate Enlightenment canons of knowledge by dynamically linking the realms of science and fiction," but the mechanism Bender identifies for how the novel did so – by "setting [science and fiction] in opposition" – merits further examination. For Bender, "science needs separation of its findings and procedures from the ordinary" and "cannot tolerate the imputation of fictionality," "hence induction emerges as the opposite of hypothesis in scientific method because it attains or seems to attain independence from the fictional" (Bender,

1998, pp. 8–9). This separation of the fictional and inductive makes sense as a heuristic for distinguishing between fiction and hypothesis, but in the case of fiction it is perhaps more about – in Bender's formulation – what "seems." The world of the "as if" in the eighteenth-century novel is not factual even if similar – in its strategies of representation – to how virtual witnessing helped produce matters of scientific fact. However, novels both invite and illustrate inductive inferences, often with a focus on processes of reasoning through the "as if." Many novels – particularly the ones I call novels of data – "present attributes of inductive proof" and "force readers into the position of neutral observers arriving, probabilistically, at judgments based upon the weight of available facts and reasonable inferences," as Bender rightly observes (Bender, 1998, p. 9). But what separates novelistic thought experiment from experimental natural philosophy is neither a strategy of representation nor an inductive *thought* process. It's rather the concept or circumstantial objective of fictionality (as Bender notes), plus the ability to query any truth claims made in fiction by way of an inductive empirical method. In short, induction is fundamental to fiction as well as to natural philosophy. Inductive inference plays an important role in fictional worlds as well as in reality, and in reality – for readers of fiction – by virtue of the former.

In eighteenth-century fiction, portrayals of or inducements to inductive reasoning mainly demonstrated how inductive empiricism might work in the social world, as opposed to investigations of the natural world. This is partially compatible with Bender's understanding of the novelistic mechanism of validating Enlightenment knowledge by setting science and fiction in opposition. As Bender writes:

> The novel, while in the main sharing verisimilar reference with empiricist science, responded to the crisis by abandoning claims to literal, historical fact of the kind Defoe had worked so strenuously to maintain and, by asserting its own manifest fictionality, strove, as Michael McKeon and Catherine Gallagher suggest, toward the representation of higher truths and toward a more intense emotional identification between readers and novelistic fictions. This novelistic occupation of the terrain of fiction then could ground the factuality of experiment in science … (Bender, 1998, p. 15).

I say partially compatible because the social focus of novelistic portrayals of induction largely cedes to natural philosophy the epistemic ground of making truth claims about the natural world by means of verisimilar representation and virtual witnessing. What's not compatible between my account of the novel and Bender's here – and McKeon's and Gallaghers's accounts by proxy – is the idea that the novel abandons its positive epistemic function in its pivot toward "representation of higher truths" and "intense emotional identification between readers and novelistic fictions" (Bender, 1998, p. 15).

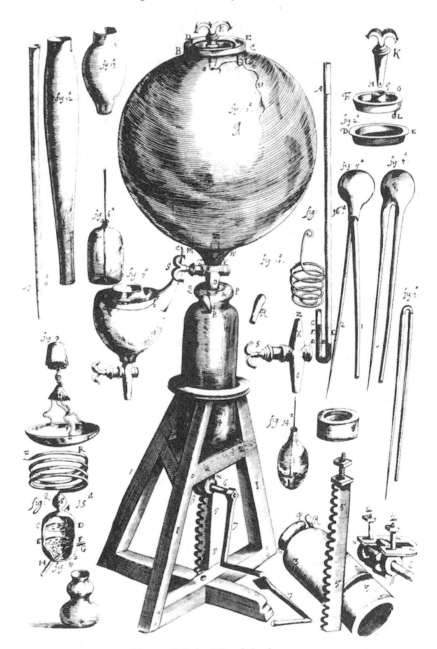

Figure 3 Robert Boyle's air-pump

I suggested earlier that a negative externality of the narrow focus on empiricism in the novel as a function of the problem of correspondence plus the problem of representation is that reasoning drops out of the picture, and this is an example of how that can happen. If we find, as Bender does, that novelistic realism was never up to the task of producing empirical knowledge by representing the real, it can appear as though that's the end of the story between the novel and empirical knowledge, or that the novel only contributed to empirical knowledge by and of a kind of failure, a negative example of knowledge production. This negative example of knowledge production Bender calls fiction (as opposed to hypothesis).

But representations of and inducements to inductive reasoning in the eighteenth-century British novel served empirical knowledge in another way. The novel's beginning preoccupations with the moral, and eventual turn toward the sentimental, run parallel to the novel's sustained demonstration of the value of inductive empiricism for *social* knowledge. Further, as I discuss in Section 4, history and philosophy of science have increasingly demonstrated the relevance of social reasoning and social knowledge to *all* forms of empirical knowledge production.

The negative externality of undervaluing reasoning in the novel has an unfortunate corollary I noted earlier (and this is worth expounding). Any marginalization of the eighteenth-century British novel's epistemic virtues is also the marginalization of the role of women in the history of empiricist theories of knowledge. Another way of putting this is that because so many eighteenth-century novels were written by women, who were kept on the margins of natural philosophy, the novel was frequently a work of philosophy in its own right. In the most prominent, even recent, histories of philosophy – taking A. C. Grayling's (2019) offering as an example – you will not find entries on women in the sections on seventeenth- and eighteenth-century empiricism. Again, because literature scholars tend not to study novels as philosophical works, and philosophers tend not to study novels much at all, women's contributions to eighteenth-century empiricism are underrepresented both in the history of the novel and in the history of philosophy. The gendering of the disciplines – from the seventeenth-century Royal Society's view of natural philosophy as a masculine endeavor to today's association of scientific knowledge with "hard" facts literature with "soft skills" or "emotional intelligence" – only compounds this problem (we can observe in today's defenses of literature as quarry of "emotional intelligence" the resonance of the Bender, McKeon, and Gallagher account of the novel's sentimental turn as a departure from matters of empirical knowledge).

Two of the three novels I discuss in what follows were written by women who were keen social epistemologists: Charlotte Lennox and Frances Burney. I might have added Jane Austen, whose novels – particularly *Sense and Sensibility* (1811), initially drafted during the 1790s – are full of insights about induction, heavily concerned with how to move from minute observations to general rules.[1] Instead I chose to keep the primary texts of this study strictly within the eighteenth century proper. Given the scope and purpose of the Elements format, the novels I've chosen are meant to be exemplary of some important ways novels engaged questions of empirical knowledge, rather than comprehensive of all the things novels did and all the ways they contributed to empirical knowledge in the eighteenth century. I've selected and ordered them chronologically – one novel from the early century, one from the mid, and one from the late – but their order also reflects a conversation throughout the century about representing, questioning, and trusting empirical knowledge.

Section 1 offers a philosophical overview of eighteenth-century theories of knowledge as context for the discussions in Sections 2, 3, and 4. Section 2, on Daniel Defoe's *Robinson Crusoe* (1719), considers the novel of data. Section 3, on Charlotte Lennox's *The Female Quixote* (1752), considers the novel of perception. And Section 4, on Frances Burney's *Evelina* (1778), considers the novel of testimony. Other novels make appearances in these sections, but the above three novels are the main, exemplary texts of this study. What draws these novels together in their treatment of questions of empirical knowledge is how they address foundational aspects of knowing. The novel of data collapses observation and representation as a strategy for foregrounding processes and methods of thought. The novel of perception does the opposite, raising intractable problems of empirical observation to demonstrate how to reason through such problems. The novel of testimony brings these considerations together into a thought experiment about gaining experience in and knowledge of the world – particularly the social world – with a practical focus on how we allocate credibility and make sound judgments from testimony.

One final caveat before proceeding to the sections: given the central objective of this Element, I have narrowed my readings of the primary texts to matters of epistemic relevance. I do not offer exhaustive or comprehensive readings of *Robinson Crusoe*, *The Female Quixote*, and *Evelina*; my aim is not to produce a reading of these driven by what Elaine Auyoung (via Peter Lipton) calls "lovely" inferences, inferences valued for their ability to help us "perceive coherence within a text" (Auyoung, 2020, p. 105). Instead I draw attention to rather typical – that is, not anomalous – features and vignettes in each novel to show how they reflect or interact with questions of empirical knowledge. Where I discuss one example, you will find many like it in the novel. And where I linger on such examples, you will find I inevitably neglect passages that may speak to other scholarly or critical concerns, or other

---

[1] For more on Austen's contributions to inductive and deductive inference, see Hanlon (forthcoming c).

prominent lines of inquiry in these novels. I admire Auyoung's incisive observation that scholars of literature operate according to "implicit values and conventions that shape the readings we produce," and "which have not yet been subject to serious disciplinary reflection." These values include, in particular, "privileging certain reading goals and domains of background knowledge over others," "pursuing interpretive inferences that have significant explanatory power regardless of their probability," and "valuing the discovery of new patterns for organization textual information as an end in itself, even when we are unpersuaded by accompanying claims about why these new ordering principles are significant" (Auyoung, 2020, p. 94). For these reasons I've made an effort here to be transparent about my reading objectives – which are primarily epistemic – as well as the kinds of examples and inferences I'm likely to attend to, and why. My contention, however, is that even if you're reading this without much interest in eighteenth-century theories of knowledge but with general interest in encountering three canonical eighteenth-century novels in new ways, my focus on the novel's capacity for reasoning through problems of empirical knowledge is already a new way of reading these novels. In other words, the sheer ordinariness of the examples I attend to – and the likelihood that where I consider one example, you can point to others that function similarly – demonstrates the extent to which staging inferential reasoning structured countless other topics and mechanisms in the eighteenth-century novel.

1 Eighteenth-Century Theories of Knowledge

Two considerations converged at the center of eighteenth-century theory of knowledge in Britain: the rise of empiricism and the basis of inference. The ascendency of empiricist theories of knowledge in the seventeenth and eighteenth centuries drew attention to two generative problems in particular. The first is the problem of perception, that ideas and workings of the mind mediate between us and the world. This raised an important set of questions, such as how we can know if our thoughts accurately represent the outside world and whether indeed there is a knowable outside world beyond our perception. John Locke largely left open this "veil of perception" problem for eighteenth-century empiricists, most notably George Berkeley and David Hume, to address. The second is the problem of induction, most famously posed by Hume in *A Treatise of Human Nature* (1739) and invoked again in *An Enquiry Concerning Human Understanding* (1748). The problem of induction concerns the question of how we generalize from empirical observation, and on what grounds.

As I explained in the introduction, scholars of the novel, particularly as it relates to empiricist thought, have focused on the relationship between perception and representation, since this is most obviously at stake in the study of novelistic realism as formal realism, a set of strategies for representing the world in writing. Realism has been the basis of longstanding claims that the eighteenth-century rise of the novel was an epistemic event, or that there was something particular to the novel genre that made it capable of conveying knowledge or participating in emerging forms of knowledge production in the seventeenth and eighteenth centuries. Scholars have typically understood realism in the eighteenth-century novel as a formal claim to verisimilitude – to a particular way of representing things as they are – which has led to two influential conclusions in the study of novelistic realism. One is that problems of perception are also problems of realism. In other words, even if, as Henry Fielding put it in *Tom Jones* (Fielding,1749, p. 352), "every good author will confine himself within the bounds of probability," the novel's epistemic status would seem contingent upon how we perceive and represent the probable. The other is that the novel's formal means of representation are the bases for understanding whether a novel meets the philosophical standards of empiricism. As Jonathan Kramnick notes, "most but not all philosophers of the seventeenth and eighteenth centuries had some sort of representational theory of mind" in which "the mind works by forming representations of objects and events and then implementing them in various processes of thought" (Kramnick, 2010, p. 264). An interest in comparing novelistic strategies of representation with empiricist theories of mind has led scholars to focus on matters of perception and representation in tandem.[2]

This section will touch on empiricism as a matter of perception and representation, but will further address matters of inference as they bear on eighteenth-century theories of knowledge. To contextualize the relationship between empiricism and inference, I begin in the seventeenth century, with three of the most influential models for eighteenth-century theories of knowledge: those of Francis Bacon, Rene Descartes, and John Locke.

In one sense, Bacon's empiricism – based in the view that knowledge comes through or must be tested by appeal to sensory experience – and Descartes's rationalism – based in the view that knowledge comes only from rational inference – are opposing theories of knowledge, the former an inductive method and the latter a deductive method. In eighteenth-century Britain,

---

[2] In addition to Watt (1957) and Bender (2012), see McKeon (2000), Keiser (2020), Lupton (2012), and Kramnick (2010).

versions of Baconian empiricism won out. As Dahlia Porter observes, "other methodological approaches existed, even flourished, but Baconian induction and the empiricist tradition spawned by Locke's *Essay* underwrote much of the conceptual orientation of later seventeenth- and eighteenth-century natural and moral philosophy" (Porter, 2018, p. 4).

Nevertheless, elements of Cartesian skepticism would inform refinements of Baconian and Lockean empiricism in the eighteenth century, including in the work of Berkeley and Hume. For Descartes, ascertaining certainty of a first principle through a method of doubt or skepticism was paramount, since his method relied on working deductively from first principles (Grayling, 2019, pp. 198, 201). Similarly, Berkeley and Hume would scrutinize the first principle behind Locke's veil of perception – that we cannot be sure of the external world because our senses and intellection can never give us a perfect account of it – rendering perception and representational theories of the mind prominent areas of inquiry in eighteenth-century empiricism. As Alex Wragge-Morley observes, "when he first framed the argument that knowledge could only result from the possession of 'clear and distinct' mental ideas," Descartes "modeled his account of knowledge on an apparently subjective description of the mental clarity arising from persuasive acts of speech," a consideration taken up by Royal Society inductive empiricists such as John Wilkins. The Royal Society "valued pictures – whether produced graphically or verbally – chiefly for their capacity to elicit the cognitively beneficial pleasure associated with the possession of clear and distinct ideas" (Wragge-Morley, 2020, pp. 15, 20). Further, as Wragge-Morley points out, "Locke's account [of primary versus secondary qualities] closely resembles arguments made by both [Robert] Boyle and Rene Descartes concerning the differences between our sensory perceptions and the real qualities from which those perceptions spring" (Wragge-Morley, 2020, p. 122). Descartes influenced both seventeenth- and eighteenth-century empiricists in this way, suggesting that knowledge relies on clear ideas – which are partly a function of language choices – and that sensory perception is not enough for knowledge; we also have to draw inferences from impressions in the mind derived from sensory experience.

How to process the written word was an important consideration for empiricists. Locke – and the eighteenth-century readers and writers he influenced, such as Samuel Johnson – understood reading as a form of inferential reasoning, as opposed to a delivery mechanism either for verisimilar accounts of or experiential engagements with nature. As Harriet Kirkley writes of Locke's "Some Thoughts Concerning Reading and Study for a Gentleman" (1739), "what [Locke] called understanding develops in three stages, as a form of inferential critical reasoning. First, one chooses a body of reading appropriate for the desired end; second, one attends to 'the connection of these Ideas in the propositions, which those books hold forth, and pretend to teach as truths' . . . The third, most important stage is that of reasoning from connected propositions to a writer's underlying premises" (Kirkley, 2002, p. 168).

Notably, this idea of reading as inferential reasoning was not confined to reading particular genres of writing, such as natural philosophy. In the *Novum Organum*, Bacon personifies "experience" as being "taught to read and write" and "having learned her letters" (Qtd. in Porter, 2018, p. 38). For both Locke and Bacon, inductive reasoning is an expressly textual process, relying on the use of writing as well as tabulation to record and organize thoughts and observations from which to reason. This is central to Locke's general theory of knowledge, for which "ideas" and "words" are "the great instruments of knowledge" and knowledge itself is "the perception of the connexion and agreement, or disagreement and repugnancy, of any of our ideas" (Qtd. in Grayling, 2019, p. 222). Locke's idea of "judgment," "the mind's capacity for distinguishing between the ideas generated by sensation," was greatly aided by the ability to organize thoughts in writing (Wragge-Morley, 2020, p. 131).

Locke goes on to describe what he calls "sensitive knowledge" in the final book of the *Essay Concerning Human Understanding* (1690), the "perception of the mind, employed about the particular existence of finite beings outside us, which going beyond bare probability and yet not reaching perfectly to either of the foregoing degrees of certainty, passes under the name of knowledge" (Qtd. in Grayling, 2019, p. 223). According to Locke's theory of perception, things have "primary qualities," which are "in things themselves," and "secondary qualities," which are how things appear to us via our senses (Qtd. in Grayling, 2019, p. 220). The disjunction between these produces the contradiction that "if Locke's official [rationalist] definition of knowledge is correct, then sensitive knowledge is impossible; and if sensitive knowledge is possible, then Locke's official definition of knowledge must fall" (Rickless, 2008, p. 83).

Locke's category of sensitive knowledge is empirical knowledge. What he calls "intuitive knowledge," "the perception of the connexion and agreement, or disagreement and repugnancy, of any of our ideas," does not conflict with Cartesian rationalism (Qtd. in Grayling, 2019, p. 222). Locke's theory of knowledge left open the possibility not only of a rationalist account of knowledge as "intuitive knowledge," but also the need to refine his description of empirical or "sensitive knowledge," which by Locke's account is relatively reliable but not certain. Fundamental to Locke's empiricism is the belief that it is impossible to know for sure that a sensory experience gives us access to a thing's primary qualities (Wragge-Morley, 2020, p. 123). This in turn opened the door for eighteenth-century empiricists to address not only perception and representation, but also how we reason from sense data, given that the mind is always mediating between what we can know of the world around us, such that experience alone is insufficient for empirical knowledge.

George Berkeley's eighteenth-century contributions to empiricist philosophy arise largely in response to Locke's veil of perception. As an empiricist, Berkeley recognized that Locke's description of sensitive knowledge was vulnerable to the skeptical challenge that knowledge of a world outside of perception is impossible since our perceptual apparatus will always make it impossible to distinguish between appearance and reality. He opened *A Treatise Concerning the Principles of Human Knowledge* (Berkeley, 1710) by addressing the skeptical view that "the faculties we have are few, and those designed by nature for the support and comfort of life, and not to penetrate the inward essence and constitution of things." "But, perhaps," Berkeley goes on, "we may be too partial to ourselves in placing the fault originally in our faculties, and not rather in the wrong use we make of them" (Berkeley, 1710, pp. 7–8). Here he moves to question the very assumption of a gap between what exists and what we perceive through our senses and experience in our minds.

Berkeley's way of answering the skeptic's challenge to Locke's veil of perception was to let go of the idea of a world "out there" in the first place, to take the immaterialist position that matter itself does not exist. "Some truths there are so near and obvious to the mind that a man need only open his eyes to see them," writes Berkeley. He contends that among these too-obvious truths is that "all those bodies which compose the mighty frame of the world, have not any substance without a mind," hence "not any other substance than spirit, or that which perceives." Berkeley reaches this conclusion by considering that the "sensible qualities" of color, figure, motion, smell, and taste are all "ideas perceived by sense," unavailable to any "unperceiving thing," thus not made of any "unthinking substance or substratum of those ideas" (Berkeley, 1710, p. 26). In short, for Berkeley, empiricism is grounded in the experience of sense perception – as it is for Locke – but what we perceive, the "bodies which compose the mighty frame of the world," are not composed of matter, but of sensible qualities or ideas. In this model, the matter is supererogatory to any explanation of what we perceive and why, so Berkeley sees no reason to believe that what we experience is based on matter rather than ideas. For Berkeley, ideas are things.

Like Locke and Berkeley, Hume carries forward the empiricist view that knowledge is rooted in experience, starting with a position compatible with Berkeley's immaterialism but without embracing that conclusion. For Hume, our perceptions are divided into "impressions" and "ideas." Impressions are "our more lively perceptions when we hear, or see, or feel, or love, or hate, or desire, or will." Hume distinguishes impressions from ideas, "which are the less lively perceptions, of which we are conscious, when we reflect on any of those sensations or movements above mentioned" (Hume, 1748, pp. 12–13). Hume does not mean "impressions" in the sense of things out in the world stamping or impressing upon our minds; impressions are rather like data points in the mind that we connect together through "resemblance" (similarity), "contiguity" (multiple thoughts occurring at the same time, which we are naturally inclined put together), and "cause or effect." Like the others, this last form of connection – cause or effect – Hume takes as a natural property of the human mind, an ingrained tendency to order things in such a way. The organizing principle of cause or effect is what takes Hume from his theory of impressions – which is compatible with Berkeley's immaterialism – to his explanation for why we believe in the existence of things in the world extrinsic to perception: our minds are wired to understand a cause in the world leading to an effect in the mind (Grayling, 2019, p. 245).

The strength of causal thinking for Hume is related to his belief in the human capacity for inductive inference; we infer what is true. In the chain of empiricist thought from Bacon and Locke to Berkeley and Hume, Hume brings the matter of induction back into focus. The principal divide between Baconian empiricist theories of knowledge and Cartesian rationalist theories of knowledge is inductive argument (for the former) in which the conclusion does not follow from the premises and deductive argument (for the latter) in which the conclusion follows from the premises. Hume famously recognized a logical flaw in induction even as he acknowledged that inductive reasoning is fundamentally how we make our way through the world. Articulating the problem of induction, Hume writes:

> The bread, which I formerly eat, nourished me; that is, a body of such sensible qualities was, at that time, endued with such secret powers: but does it follow, that other bread must also nourish me at another time, and that like sensible qualities must always be attended with like secret powers? The consequence seems nowise necessary. At least, it must be acknowledged that there is here a consequence drawn by the mind; that there is a certain step taken; a process of thought, and an inference, which wants to be explained
> (Hume, 1748, pp. 24–25).

Yet acknowledging that we successfully rely on inductive leaps, he writes:

> These two propositions are far from being the same, *I have found that such an object has always been attended with such an effect*, and *I foresee, that other objects, which are, in appearance, similar, will be attended with similar*

effects. I shall allow, if you please, that the one proposition may justly be inferred from the other: I know, in fact, that it always is inferred. But if you insist that the inference is made by a chain of reasoning, I desire you to produce that reasoning. The connexion between these propositions is not intuitive. There is required a medium, which may enable the mind to draw such an inference, if indeed it be drawn by reasoning and argument. What that medium is, I must confess, passes my comprehension; and it is incumbent on those to produce it, who assert that it really exists, and is the origin of all our conclusions concerning matter of fact (Hume, 1748, pp. 24–25).

In brief, the practical method for coming to knowledge that Bacon advocated becomes similarly for Hume "the origin of all our conclusions concerning matter of fact," the basis for empirical knowledge. Only the burden is on one making the inference to justify it, unlike a validly deductive proposition that necessarily follows from its premises. For Hume, as Porter observes, "even if authors did not follow a strictly inductive approach in their research or writing, the value of induction for producing knowledge as text remained a salient rhetorical stance throughout the seventeenth- and eighteenth-century natural and moral philosophy" (Porter, 2018, p. 40).

Porter's observation about Hume is crucial for understanding the role of the eighteenth-century novel in the history of empiricism. Arriving at knowledge through the Baconian framework of inductive empiricism, the dominant theory of knowledge in the period, required more than offering or illustrating theories of perception and representation. It also required methods of reasoning or conceptual methods. As Porter observes, "in the seventeenth and eighteenth centuries, 'method' referred both to procedures of data accumulation and to the mental operations of sorting and organizing" (Porter, 2018, p. 35). "Methods" of knowledge production also entailed ideas about organizing thoughts and justifying inferences. The novel's engagement with seventeenth- and eighteenth-century empiricism certainly included illustrating problems of perception and strategies of reliable representation – as I will show in discussions of Daniel Defoe's *Robinson Crusoe* (1719) and Charlotte Lennox's *The Female Quixote* (1752), among others – but novels frequently dwelled on the methods by which we reason and draw conclusions beyond the point of apprehension and perception and despite the challenges of representation. Further, because Hume's influential theory of knowledge involved a "shift of evidentiary base" from discussions of the particulars of observation and experiment to discussions of the particulars of texts – examples from history and poetry – the problem of induction could be staged not just in texts of natural and moral philosophy, but also in texts of narrative fiction and nonfiction. As Porter writes, "the laws of both criticism and cognition could be generated inductively from the existing databank of literary texts" (Porter, 2018, p. 53).

From the beginning, the Baconian method that would guide much of seventeenth and eighteenth-century empiricist thought entailed more than working out problems of perception and representation; it was also explicitly engaged in questions of how to reason from observation, or how to reason inductively. Notwithstanding what A. C. Grayling calls the "caricature" of Baconian empiricism embraced by Isaac Newton and Charles Darwin, among others – that Bacon's empiricism meant gathering random observations, then fitting a theory to them – the purpose of gathering observations is to test an antecedent hypothesis. As Bacon writes in *The Novum Organum* (1620), "for induction by simple enumeration is childish and precarious. But true induction analyses nature by rejections and exclusions, and concludes affirmatively after a sufficient number of negatives. And our greatest hope rests upon this way of induction" (Bacon, 1620, p. 228). Bacon's inductive method and its eighteenth-century reformulations in empiricist theories of knowledge required not just an examination of how the mind apprehends, processes, interprets, and experiences sensory input, but also of how we ought to reason and draw conclusions from the aggregation of sense data. Eighteenth-century novels frequently picked up this line of inquiry. Bacon's theory of knowledge stressed that knowledge must be useful, which meant developing methods for reaching reliable conclusions and providing sound explanations. Novels that illustrate the stakes of reliable inference for their characters, such as Arabella in *The Female Quixote*, put methods of reasoning into practical attire for their readers.

For empiricism to continue to develop into a useful knowledge program, then, eighteenth-century thought needed to address not only the role of fiction in hypothesizing, but also more granular matters of reasoning from sense data, and this is where the novel excelled. Hume's recognition that the problem of induction required explanation even beyond a probable account of the relative reliability of the senses meant that even if one were to solve the veil of perception problem, the need for a method of inductive reasoning would remain. This is the case whether or not we believe – as do many philosophers today – that Hume's "argument against induction is irrefutable on its own terms," since Hume was clear that despite the problem we regularly rely on inductive arguments (Okasha, 2001, p. 307). On this point it is perhaps worth mentioning that in the essay "Of the Standard of Taste" (1757) Hume compared the development of moral sense with the practice of literary criticism, as both require careful attention to and detailed observations about our objects of consideration and with these a continual refining of the faculty of judgment. Though Hume goes on to admit that such a mechanism of judgment does not apply so easily to moral principles in the world, especially to changing moral attitudes, eighteenth-century novels provide evidence of fiction foregrounding arguments about morality and taste, credibility and rationale, and exercising methods of reasoning in the process. Central to this feature of the eighteenth-century novel is the emergent concept of "data," the raw materials novels collected to stage problems of inferential reasoning.

2 The Novel of Data

In eighteenth-century Britain, data and the novel rose together. As Daniel Rosenberg shows, "the word 'data' entered the English language in the seventeenth century and was naturalized in the eighteenth" (Rosenberg, 2013, p. 32). Throughout the eighteenth century, "data" referred to particulars across a range of knowledge domains and in several different forms. Henry Hammond used the term to describe a collection of theological propositions in *A Brief Vindication of Three Passages in the Practical Catechisme* (1646). Joseph Priestley used it in *Lectures on History and General Policy* (1788) to describe historical facts and again in *Experiments and Observations on Different Kinds of Air* (1777) to refer to experimental measurements (Rosenberg, 2013, pp. 20, 15, 17). As early as 1630, in *A Most Plaine and Easie Way for Finding the Sunne's Amplitude and Azimuth* (1630), William Batten referred to a table of figures conveying a ship's position (for the purpose of demonstrating a navigational calculation) as "data," indicating that "data" could refer to givens in mathematics as well (Batten, 1630, p. 5). By 1701, George Cheyne used "data" to describe observations made about the workings of the body from which to develop medical treatment (Cheyne, 1701, p. iv). Likewise in 1701, John Arbuthnot called for "sufficient *data* and decisive Experiments" for understanding the "internal motions" of the body (Arbuthnot, 1701, p. 18).

Ranging in context and application, these usages of "data" tell a common story about its rhetorical and epistemic status, the story of the given or granted. As Rosenberg rightly cautions, data and evidence aren't interchangeable concepts, though calling evidence "data" – as in Hammond's theological evidence and Cheyne and Arbuthnot's anatomical evidence – was often a rhetorical gesture to signal the givenness of the evidence. That which is given is to be taken for granted, not to be questioned. In this sense, "data" might be indicative of a thought experiment or mathematical exercise, as when Batten offers hypothetical figures for a ship's position to be used in the exercise of calculating azimuth. But "data" might also indicate, as for Cheyne and Arbuthnot, empirical evidence or observations from which to make inferences about how things work, not to be questioned on account of the integrity granted to observation as a way of knowing. In the early-eighteenth century, "data" more often referred to the axiomatic, but by the end of the century it was more commonly used to refer to observed particulars gathered in experiment or collection (Rosenberg, 2013, p. 33). The rise of empiricism occasioned new disciplinary and evidentiary developments. As Rosenberg writes, "the rise of modern economics and empirical natural science created new conditions of argument and new assumptions about facts and evidence," which explains the shift from "data" as axiomatic to "data" as empirical as the latter emerged as an evidentiary standard (Rosenberg, 2013, p. 36).

As Lorraine Daston and Peter Galison observe, "just as the methods of experiment or of statistical inference, once invented and established, survive the demise of various scientific theories, so epistemic virtues, once entrenched, seem to endure," with the new ones modifying the old (Daston and Galison, 2007, p. 41). The change in epistemic standards that Rosenberg, Daston and Galison, and Mary Poovey have all documented did not obviate the need for systems of inference or supplant it with some kind of numerical objectivity, but it did modify how natural philosophers addressed longstanding problems of inference and observation.[3] Writing of Samuel Johnson's account of the Scottish Highlands, Poovey notes that "when Johnson synecdochically generalizes both his own 'eye' and its responses, it becomes plain that what he initially presented as a self-evident inference is a subjective response informed by reading, experience, and temperament" (Poovey, 1998, p. 252). Similarly, Daston and Galison find that objectivity – what they term "seeing without inference" – is actually contingent upon "the integrity of the self, as well as that of scientific observations and the inferences drawn from them" (Daston and Galison, 2007, pp. 17, 235). Rosenberg's study of the eighteenth-century emergence of the concept of data emphasizes the specifically rhetorical nature of that concept as the word "data" found its way into the discourse of natural philosophy.

The rhetorical value of calling something "data" carried with it an epistemological assumption, even if, as Rosenberg concisely puts it, "facts are ontological, evidence is epistemological, data is rhetorical" (Rosenberg, 2013, p. 18). We're not meant to question data because its givenness is either axiomatic or observational. Both rationales for the epistemic givenness of data are pertinent to the eighteenth-century novel. For the former, because it is through conceiving of minute particulars as givens that novels can stage thought experiments about situations that resemble life as it is or the physical word as it is, such that characters and readers make judgments and inferences about the data presented.

In this sense what is widely understood as novelistic realism based in verisimilitude – and in strategies of representation aimed at conveying

---

[3] For more on this topic, particularly its role in the present-day promotion of numerical or quantitative evidence, see Porter (1995) and Deringer (2018).

impressions of the real – does not itself constitute empirical knowledge or a particular lease on the real. Instead, it forms a realistic training ground for inference. The judgments and inferences we make from novels require us to take what the novel represents as axiomatic without taking novel representations as empirically true (unlike Don Quixote, we do not take fictional representations for facts of the world; we take them as thought experiments). Novelistic data in this (axiomatic) sense is similar to Batten's given figures for an instructive exercise in navigational calculation. It doesn't matter whether Batten's figures were originally derived from an extant ship and its true geospatial position for us to make use of them as examples for learning navigational calculations. Similarly, novelistic realism offers fictional data as a pedagogical exercise, a training ground for inference through which authors can highlight pitfalls of perception and reasoning and sometimes offer solutions. In this way the novel brought together the axiomatic and empirical senses of data because novelistic realism drew on the emergent authority of empiricism to present representations as givens. Bender rightly identifies novelistic verisimilitude as a form of what Shapin and Schaffer call "virtual witnessing," "the production in a *reader's* mind of such an image of an experimental scene as obviates the necessity for either direct witness or replication" (Bender, 1998, p. 8; Shapin and Schaffer, 2011 p. 60). However, unlike the scientific atlases that employed virtual witnessing, novels, as Catherine Gallagher notes, were "believable stories that did not solicit belief" (Gallagher, 2006, p. 340).

Understanding realistic representation in the eighteenth-century novel specifically as data – and in the context of the emergence of "data" as an epistemic term in the period – adds an important perspective to the familiar picture of novelistic realism as formal strategies of verisimilitude. For Gallagher, "fictionality only became visible when it became credible, because it only needed conceptualizing as the difference between fictions and lies became less obvious" (Gallagher, 2006, p. 340). And for Bender, the novel's "fictionality plays a role in certifying reality," "linking the realms of science and fiction in the very process of setting them in opposition" (Bender, 1998, pp. 21, 6). In both accounts, novelistic realism offered a break with actual truth claims by legitimating the idea that forms of representation themselves cannot be epistemically reliable, or that truth lies in form. But if we understand novelistic representation as data, we understand that *all* realistic representations across knowledge domains are insufficient for knowledge production; all are provisional givens. Both empiricism and novelistic representation actually needed the same thing: not formal innovations or more realistic ways of representing the real, but an acceptance of data as a collection of provisional givens, and a method for drawing inferences from those givens. In other words, knowledge becomes "certified," in Bender's sense of the term, not in opposition to novelistic fiction, but through the recognition that even the real requires fictional – that is, inductive – leaps, a system of thought for connecting the dots. A more concise way of saying this is that the novel's primary innovation wasn't formal, but methodological. The novel took up the emergent epistemology of data.

On this point it is important to note that while the novel and novelistic representation played an important role in the development of the concept of data in eighteenth-century Britain, the novel did not represent data in any unique way. Despite the influence of Watt's realist thesis, it's implausible to argue that the novel had any particular generic claim to strategies of verisimilitude. Mary Baine Campbell suggests that Hooke's "*Micrographia* is *more* highly plotted, more artificially *shaped* than other works in its genre and thus functions more easily to channel features of style or perception into more characteristically shapely and plotted genres like the novel" (Campbell, 1999, p. 201). Yet it is not clear that what makes *Micrographia* (1665a) "a forerunner to *Pamela's* minute invoices of the sensible world" is a common "shape" so much as a common epistemological interest in building general propositions – whether natural or moral – from a foundation of describing or tabulating minute particulars. Recognizing this shared epistemological interest between the scientific atlas and the novel – which entails a shift in emphasis from form or "shape" to epistemology and methods of reasoning – helps us see how the eighteenth-century novel was an inferential system in its own right, neither a genre wholly derivative of seventeenth-century natural philosophy nor in possession of unique strategies of realist representation. Whether minute description, listing, interpolated numerical figures, illustrations, figurative language, or the rhetoric of immediacy, what we find in eighteenth-century novels we also find in scientific atlases, navigational treatises, land surveying documents, life writing, and other prominent genres of the period. Beyond verisimilitude, the main thing the novel contributed to empirical knowledge was the staging ground for thought experiments in how to reason from data that was to be taken, if only provisionally or hypothetically, as given.

For example, the rhetorical use of immediacy – in the language of eighteenth-century empiricists, the "immediately perceived" or the "immediate object of perception," and in the language of Hooke's description of his stinging nettle experiment, "*presently* after I had thrust them in" [emphasis mine] – functions across genres like the rhetorical use of "data." Both are efforts to give the impression of having seen through Locke's veil of perception, or of a narrowed if not closed epistemic gap between what is seen and known, what is seen and represented, and what is represented and known. In this way, novels participated in and worked through two intellectual traditions of the period: the empirical

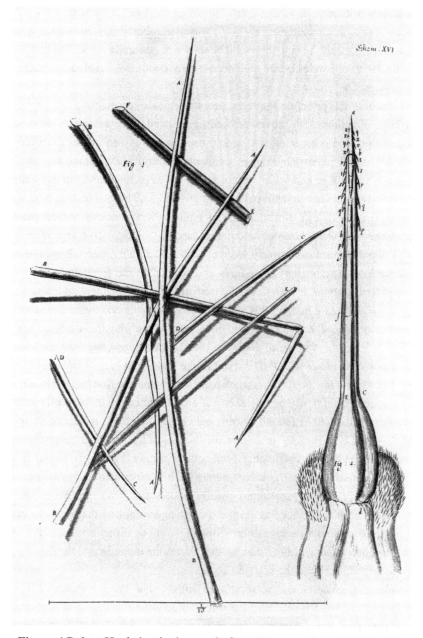

Figure 4 Robert Hooke's stinging nettle from *Micrographia*, 1665 (Hooke, 1665b) (licensed under **CC BY 4.0**)

basis of knowledge and, consequently, the elevation of data – the aggregation of minute particulars taken as givens – to the upper echelon of evidentiary forms. "Data" retained its rhetorical function throughout the eighteenth century (and retains it today, as when we say "show me the data" or "the data show[s]" as an appeal to conclusiveness), but it was also increasingly associated with forms of evidence, the kind that could be shown or gestured toward. The novel – particularly for Daniel Defoe – evinced awareness of this developing evidentiary standard.

Of course, this principle of intergeneric strategies of representing data applies in both directions. The novel certainly employed plain language, detailed description, and other strategies widely used in the written genres of experimental natural philosophy, but experimental natural philosophers also used figurative language and other strategies that we have since come to associate with literature. This point is widely established but bears mention here as essential context. Experimental natural philosophers famously valued plain language and were cautious about the capacity of figurative language to mislead when used excessively, even as they relied on figurative language in accounts of experimental procedures and results. In the foregoing example from *Micrographia*, Hooke describes performing an experiment on himself – applying a stinging nettle to his skin – in both dramatic and figurative terms: "presently after I had thrust them in I felt the burning pain begin; next I observ'd in divers of them, that upon thrusting my finger against their tops, the Bodkin (if I may so call it) did not in the least bend ... " (Hooke, 1665a, p. 143). Were it lineated, with its meter and end rhyme, the first part of Hooke's description could easily be mistaken for a rhyming couplet: "presently after I had thrust them in / I felt the burning pain begin." Hooke's metaphor for the nettle's barb is a "Bodkin" or dagger, an instance of figurative language that at once dramatizes the experiment (if the nettle's stinger is a dagger, Hooke has stabbed himself with it) and communicates his experimental procedure in a way others not present might readily understand. Had one never seen a nettle's barb magnified, as Hooke did when he applied the nettle to his skin while looking through a microscope, it would be difficult to conceive of its shape and effect without language that relates the unfamiliar to the familiar, the magnified nettle to the bodkin.

Following Shapin and Schaffer's *Leviathan and the Air-Pump* (2011), scholars have written much on the role of figurative language and narrative description in Royal Society experimental natural philosophy.[4] Tita Chico writes, for example, "observation is at once a figure and a scientific technology, and it can be so only through its reliance on imaginative work" (Chico, 2018, p. 21). Claire Preston observes that "headway in early-modern science was often analogical," such that "its insights and expression had the structure of

---

[4] See also Vickers (2002, pp. 287–335), Picciotto (2010), Smith (2016), and Chico (2018).

a rhetorical figure" (Preston, 2016, p. 5). Even in Helen Thompson's challenge to one of Shapin and Schaffer's basic theses about the early modern construction of matters of fact – that fact is a function of virtual or collective witnessing of the visible or perceptible – Thompson notes that "both scientific discourse and prose fiction . . . elaborate modes of figural, formal, and experimental access to imperceptible things," affirming the wider arguments of Shapin and Schaffer, Preston, and Chico that figurative language is intergeneric and basic to early modern science as well as the novel (Thompson, 2016, p. 3).

I chose *Robinson Crusoe* to illustrate how novels could function like data-based experiments in making inferences from minute particulars. In terms of numerical data, *Journal of the Plague Year* (1722) would also be a good case study – the obvious case study – but my aim in choosing *Robinson Crusoe* instead is to illustrate perhaps the more subtle ways the novel used verbal strategies to represent the given.[5] Defoe's novels are valuable case studies for this line of inquiry because, even as Defoe explicitly treats narrative as a means of presenting and ordering data – treating the novel as an informational genre – he also usefully refuses the assumption that plain language, tabulation, listing, and minute description offer certainty or an immediate window into the real. In fact, like *Journal*, *Robinson Crusoe* dwells in perilous uncertainty despite the efforts of its protagonist to offer plain statements of fact or reliable heuristics for sorting through all the data. What Defoe denies his protagonists is to the epistemic benefit of his readers because his protagonists model useful ways of presenting and evaluating data, reflecting a reality in which empirical knowledge is probable and provisional and we do the best we can to find our way to it. It was precisely through the aggregation of sense data – despite uncertainty of whether a sensory experience was a direct reflection of the essential qualities of things in the world – that empiricists such as Locke, Robert Boyle, and the botanist John Ray believed we could most reliably develop empirical knowledge. Ray, for example, "argued that the best way to identify species was through the enumeration and comparison of a relatively large number of the characteristics amenable to sensation," such that "the use of many characteristics would mitigate the possibility that some of them were misleading guides to the reality of things" (Wragge-Morley, 2020, p. 123). This is also the principle behind representational strategies in the novel of data.

Scholars frequently read *Robinson Crusoe* according to the widespread claim that, as Wolfram Schmidgen identifies it, "problems of ownership, appropriation, and exchange . . . shape the way Defoe represents persons, actions, and things, and that this way borrows from empiricism's close observation of

---

[5] For an account of how inference and credibility work in *Journal*, see Hanlon (forthcoming b).

ordinary realities to generate a fictional realism that represents the things of the world as quantifiable resources" (Schmidgen, 2016, p. 101). Even as recent Defoe scholarship has covered topics including colonialism, providentialism, ecology, environment, and economics, among others, the relationship between Defoe's abundant listing, enumeration, and aesthetics of what Schmidgen calls "infinite variety" and eighteenth-century empiricism is a common observation (Schmidgen, 2016, p. 103).[6] Defoe's empiricist tendencies were certainly central to Watt's explanation for the rise of the novel as well as to critiques of Watt's argument, especially in subsequent critical suspicion that Defoe's mode of representation enacts "a basic resistance to the literary representation of objectified forms of social life," producing "the most dreaded effects of the descriptive – a deadening emphasis on materiality that muffles human presence" (Schmidgen, 2001, p. 22).

Rather than understanding Defoe's tendencies toward particular forms of description and reduction as deadening or muffling human presence, I will discuss how Defoe's strategies of representation illustrate problems of inductive reasoning and invite readers to work through them. Defoe's writing is frequently an invitation to focused intellection – thinking aimed at understanding, as opposed to imagining – thus to the fundamentally human (and coincidentally Humean) problem of making sense of the world. Bridget Donnelly rightly sees Defoe's novelistic project as "participating in the tradition of skepticism toward casualty that is most frequently associated with David Hume," while Schmidgen sees *Robinson Crusoe* in particular as "a spiritual text whose hard material surfaces are ultimately wired to questions of faith and redemption" (Donnelly, 2019, p. 109; Schmidgen, 2016, p. 101). Whether Defoe's motivations are secular, religious, or both, these observations identify a link between Defoe's strategies of representation and his processual interest in how we attempt to make sense of the illusory without wholly foreclosing an inevitable uncertainty.

One could flip through *Robinson Crusoe* at random with good odds on putting a finger down on a passage featuring one of Defoe's characteristically detailed lists or chains of minute description. Consider, for example, how Crusoe describes constructing his raft out of the debris of the shipwreck:

> We had several spare Yards, and two or three large sparrs of Wood, and a spare Top-mast or two in the Ship; I resolv'd to fall to work with these, and I flung as many of them over board as I could manage for their Weight, tying every one with a Rope that they may not drive away; when this was done I went down the Ship's Side, and pulling them to me, I ty'd four of them fast

---

[6] See, for example – but by no means as an exhaustive list – Schmidgen (2001, pp. 19–39; 2016, pp. 101–126), Donnelly (2019, pp. 107–120), Loar (2019, pp. 31–53), Wood (2020, pp. 381–406), and MacDonnell (2020, pp. 1–24).

together at both Ends as well as I could, in the Form of a Raft, and laying two or three short Pieces of Plank upon them cross-ways, I found I could walk upon it very well, but that it was not able to bear any great Weight, the Pieces being too light; so I went to work, and with the Carpenter's Saw, I cut a spare Top-mast into three Lengths, and added them to my Raft . . .

(Defoe, 1719, p. 43).

Schmidgen points out that in such descriptions – here I emphasize the list that opens the passage – "the concreteness of the objects is sharply reduced as they almost completely lack individuating characteristics. In this way, Crusoe's list removes things from concrete contextualized relationships and encloses them in a zone of heightened visibility." As such, for Schmidgen, Crusoe's list "embodies a kind of zero-degree of description" (Schmidgen, 2001, pp. 21–22).

Two aspects of Defoe's listing as representational technique link it with eighteenth-century understandings of data. One, "zero-degree . . . description" is precisely the rhetorical goal of construing something as data, a rhetorical interest in closing the epistemic gap between the observed and the known and the observed and the related. In *Robinson Crusoe*, relating experiences and observations in the form of data – not necessarily as numbers, but as a collection of items that, like the shipwreck, are simply found as they were – is a representational strategy for provisionally sanctioning the givenness of what is being related. This shifts the epistemic burden in the narrative from the problem of perception that troubled Locke and subsequent empiricists in the eighteenth century to the problem of induction, or of how to generalize principles of knowledge, morality, faith, and so on from the given.

In this way Defoe's fiction was a precursor to late-century epistemological developments. When, for example, Adam Smith – who was suspicious of the listing style – wrote "all philosophical systems [are] mere inventions of the imagination, to connect together the otherwise disjointed and discordant phenomena of nature," he hinted at the necessity of inductive reasoning, or of connecting the dots of discrete data points, for empirical knowledge production (Qtd. in Siskin, 2001, p. 209). The point of novelistic realism taken as strategies of verisimilitude is less to demonstrate the real than to deflate the problem of perception, thus to provide givens with which to foreground methods of reasoning and the problem of induction.

The second aspect of Defoe's lists that connects them with the eighteenth-century emergence of data as a privileged evidentiary form is implied in Schmidgen's description of how Defoe's lists obscure the individual nature and context of their constituent items. Another way of saying "minute particular" is *datum*, a term that never amounted to much in the English language, at least compared with its plural counterpart, and for good reason. If the primary rhetorical value of data was its givenness, eighteenth-century writers and natural philosophers realized that the epistemic value of data was its plural-ness. "Data" was often treated in the singular, as a mass noun, from its beginnings in the English language ("the data" as opposed to "these data"), with recognition that a *datum* alone was of little use relative to lots of data (Rosenberg, 2013, p. 18). Again, Defoe understood this in a way that became increasingly common among natural philosophers by the latter half of the eighteenth century. Joseph Priestley, one of the Royal Society's early adopters of the term "data," took interest in what Rosenberg calls "large constellations of information," which partly explains his groundbreaking historical timelines, which sacrificed the individual contexts of historical figures and events (biography) to offer an image of the whole (data) (Rosenberg, 2013, pp. 16–17).[7] Credibility in a Baconian inductive empirical system comes in part from the aggregation of many particulars. Defoe was especially attuned to this, which helps explain why his lists and descriptions sacrifice the contexts of individual items, treating them instead as an aggregated whole. This is a hallmark of data as itself a collection of empirical givens and as a strategy for representing the given. Whereas Schmidgen sees this characteristic of Defoe's lists as creating "purely contiguous relationships between material objects," which "elides narrative elements," I see Defoe partaking of an emergent representational strategy of data presentation. The network, contiguity, or relationality of the particulars in a Defoean dataset is less important than the fact of their aggregation.

To the extent that relationships between listed items take on epistemic significance in *Robinson Crusoe*, however, the focus is on process and method. Returning to Crusoe's description of constructing his raft out of the items of the shipwreck, we can see the focus on process. As a description of actions, this passage is processual, with language ("when this was done") to signal where Crusoe is in the timeline of the task. Contributing to the sense of process in the passage is Defoe's care with justifications for each of Crusoe's actions. The size and sturdiness of Crusoe's raft are partly a function of how much weight he can bear in moving heavy materials into position (because Crusoe can't so easily work with heavier materials, his raft is less sturdy than it might be); Crusoe ties the boards he flings into the water with a rope so they don't drift away; he cuts a top-mast into lengths to fortify the raft because he finds it too light to begin

---

[7] For more on this, see Hanlon (forthcoming a).

with. We also get positional details – "down the Ship's Side"; "pulling them to me"; "at both Ends"; "cross-ways" – which, combined with the processual and justificatory details, fortify the integrity of the narrative account alongside Crusoe's fortification of the raft. The implication of this combination of listing and description of method and process is that one who has actually had the experience of building a raft under such circumstances must have had to think through such details of process, justification, and position. Such passages in *Robinson Crusoe* do not simply enact what are meant to be convincing strategies of representation to elide the epistemic gap between perception and things in the world, or between things in the world and their novelistic representation, through verisimilar accounts of the minute particular. They also illustrate the details of *process* or *method* by which one might understand how the data points fit together, enabling readers to follow and often to infer the reasoning behind Crusoe's actions, using connective terms of the sort I have above ("a function of"; "because"; "so that"; "to").

The repetition of detailed, descriptive passages throughout the novel requires readers to reflect on rationale to make sense of Defoe's dense lists and meticulously recorded actions. Shortly after Crusoe has built the raft and then "prepar'd a second Raft ... having had Experience of the first," Crusoe ventures back out to the wreck to recover more potentially useful materials. He prefaces the list with "I brought away several Things very useful to me . . .," which alone serves the narrative function of indicating what Crusoe was doing in this moment and why. Yet he continues with specifics:

> . . . as first, in the Carpenter's Stores I found two or three Bags full of Nails and Spikes, a great Skrew-Jack, a Dozen or two of Hatchets, and above all, that most useful Thing call'd a Grindstone; all these I secur'd together, with several Things belonging to the Gunner, particularly two or three Iron Crows, and two Barrels of Musquet Bullets, seven Musquets, and another fowling Piece, with some small Quantity of Powder more; a large Bag full of small Shot, and a great Roll of Sheet Lead: But this last was so Heavy, I could not hoise it up to get it over the Ship's Side (Defoe, 1719, p. 47).

Here we can see how the list functions as data, emphasizing aggregated particularity. "Particularly two or three Iron Crows, and two Barrels of Musquet Bullets ... " is a telling sentence, as Crusoe follows the descriptor "particularly" with an imprecise count ("two or three Iron Crows") followed by a precise count of the bullets and guns. Again, what matters in these moments is not the demonstration of a one-to-one relationship between the items described and a supposed reality, but the effect of having presented the account as data. In other words, whether two or three iron crows, what matters is that something is being not just counted, but aggregated. If we doubt the precision of Crusoe's account, we can have some confidence, like Ray, that the aggregation of details is giving us, on the whole, a good enough basis for reasoning to conclusions about Crusoe's process, intent, and awareness of his environment.

Counterintuitively, imprecision does not attenuate the credibility of the representation; it actually strengthens it. "Some small quantity of Powder" appears sensible, as one in Crusoe's circumstances would not be able to weigh or otherwise quantify the powder more precisely by looking at it. "Two or three" might also give the impression of someone attentive to particularity and accurate accounting yet susceptible to reasonable human errors, omissions, or memory lapses. Here imprecision functions somewhat like a person with a cheat sheet for an exam intentionally getting some of the questions wrong in an effort to minimize suspicion, to avoid an implausibly perfect result. Defoe's way of accounting for plausible human error works alongside the detail about finding a roll of sheet lead but not being able to hoist such a heavy object out of the ship to indicate or give the impression that this is not an idealized list but an account we can take, provisionally, as given. This is not to suggest that Defoe was unconcerned with realistic representation – far from it – but that in *Robinson Crusoe*, credibility is a function of representing not just things, but method and rationale.

In suggesting that the rhetorical gain of representing things in the form of data is the sense of givenness this produces, I am implying the importance of an additional concept essential to empirical knowledge production, credibility. The extent to which we can accept the givenness of data is partly a function of how credible we view its sources and the methods of its derivation, both of which require inferences about how the bigger picture offered in the data hangs together. This is why, for Defoe, detail alone ("two or three large sparrs of wood") is not enough for credibility; rationale ("tying every one with a Rope that they may not drive away") is essential as well. Indeed, scholars have long since noted that Defoe's penchant for minute description sometimes undermines the plausibility of the account, because *Robinson Crusoe* contains seemingly unintended errors and inconsistencies.[8] Further, as Geoffrey Bowker and Susan Leigh Star note, list forms can help make knowledge retrievable, but sprawling lists of details can also be impractical (Bowker and Star, 1999, p. 24). However, because Defoe combines a dense, detailed, informational style of representation with a lingering focus on rationales, his novels work particularly well as models of empirical knowledge production. The point here is not that we should take Defoe's narrative data in *Robinson Crusoe* as fact, for fact and given are not the same thing; the point is rather that the sense of provisional truth that data offers aids the novel in walking readers through the rationales and thought

---

[8] For an overview of this, see Hastings (1912, pp. 161–166).

processes necessary to interpret or make sense of the data. Even as Defoe insisted that his readership take *Robinson Crusoe* as a true story – as a history – he used looming uncertainty in his fiction to countervail any notion that knowledge is simply a matter of showing the data.

As I have suggested, Defoe's habit of supplying what looks like credible data without supplying certainty – that is, of supplying data that never speaks for itself – becomes a deft means of evaluating and inferring from data. Consider, for example, the pivotal moment in which Crusoe first sees what he believes is a human footprint in the sand, leading him to ongoing fear and torment at the thought of being vulnerable to other men on the island, possibly cannibals:

> It happen'd one Day about Noon going towards my Boat, I was exceedingly surpriz'd with the Print of a Man's naked Foot on the Shore, which was very plain to be seen in the Sand: I stood like one Thunder-struck, or as if I had seen an Apparition; I listen'd, I look'd round me, I could hear nothing, nor see any Thing, I went up to a rising Ground to look farther, I went up the Shore and down the Shore, but it was all one, I could see no other Impression but that one, I went to it again to see if there were any more, and to observe if it might not be my Fancy; but there was no Room for that, for there was exactly the very Print of a Foot, Toes, Heel, and every part of a Foot; how it came thither I knew not, nor could I in the least imagine. But after innumerable fluttering Thoughts, like a Man perfectly confus'd and out of my self, I came Home to my Fortification, not feeling, as we say, the Ground I went on, but terrify'd to the last Degree, looking behind me at every two or three Steps, mistaking every Bush and Tree, and fancying every Stump at a Distance to be a Man; nor is it possible to describe how many various Shapes my affrighted Imagination represented Things to me in, how many wild Ideas were found every Moment in my Fancy, and what strange, unaccountable Whimsies came into my Thoughts by the Way
>
> (Defoe, 1719, p. 130).

This passage draws together Defoe's characteristic descriptions of minute particulars aggregated as data with a detailed illustration of a method of reasoning, and does so while maintaining a realistic sense of the problem of perception. Defoe introduces Crusoe's first apprehension of the footprint by way of a list of potential causes for why Crusoe is wary of venturing too far from the shore on his boat: "I was so apprehensive of being hurry'd out of my Knowledge again by the Currents, or Winds, or any other Accident. But now I come to a new Scene of my Life" (Defoe, 1719, p. 130). Once Crusoe describes what he sees, we can imagine him listing and aggregating both the steps in his reaction ("I listen'd, I look'd round me, I could hear nothing, nor see any Thing, I went up to a rising Ground to look farther, I went up the Shore and down the Shore, but it was all one") and the components of his observation that confirm his impression that he is looking at a human footprint ("Toes, Heel, and every part of a Foot").

But we might also take note in this passage of its illustration of a common problem of perception in eighteenth-century empiricism and how to go about trying to solve it. In the scenario, Crusoe has made an empirical observation whose implications shock him, such that he wonders if his mind is playing tricks on him. He goes through several procedures to validate what he sees, among them an effort to distinguish between observation and fancy, or as Crusoe puts it, "how many wild Ideas were found every Moment in my Fancy." In this moment, Crusoe needs to understand, among other things, whether the match between his idea of a human foot and his observation of the print is true, or whether he is operating from a combination of memory and observation or if fancy, imagination, or even paranoia are confounding his impression. In Hume's theory of empiricism, memory and imagination were perilously similar faculties, both shaped by past experiences. Hume suggests that memories are more vivid than imaginings, but otherwise both are subject to error (we can misremember and we can inaccurately imagine something that actually happened but that we did not witness). Hume's criterion for distinguishing between the two is causal: memories are caused by impressions of the exact event remembered, whereas imaginings are not (Priest, 2007, pp. 170–171).

To work through this problem, Crusoe first attunes himself to his immediate surroundings in search of further sense data: "I stood like one Thunder-struck, or as if I had seen an Apparition; I listen'd, I look'd round me . . ." (Defoe, 1719, p. 130). Once he confirms that nothing else available to his senses suggests another human presence – even another footprint to match the single footprint he found – he begins a chain of inferences. If there is no corroborating evidence for a human presence beyond the single footprint, the footprint might be a figment of his imagination, whether its very existence or that it was made by a human (as opposed to another kind of creature). He checks this inference by looking in greater detail at the footprint, surveying its components, and finding that they all match those of a human footprint. From this he infers that it must not be his fancy intervening; that this must indeed be a human footprint: " . . . if it might not be Fancy; but there was no Room for that . . . "

Through this process of inference Crusoe comes to a probable conclusion about the footprint's existence and its being human, though crucially he is left with significant uncertainty, with questions whose answers he is in no position either to deduce or to infer. The singularity of the footprint – not the footprints one might expect from a two-legged creature, a datum refusing the status of data – heightens Crusoe's epistemic anxiety. Undoubtedly, Crusoe is experiencing anxiety of the non-epistemic sort – perhaps more of the existential sort – in this moment as well, fearing for his life at the prospect of Devil or cannibal having produced the ominous footprint. But Crusoe's epistemic anxiety only compounds his paranoia until he begins to work through the former. This lingering uncertainty about what is the case forces Crusoe to proceed with further chains of reasoning to dispel the gruesome thoughts of his imagination, spurred by fear. He imagines the Devil is with him on the island, then settles on the conclusion that it is more likely the footprint belongs to "the Savages of the main-Land over-against me, who had wander'd out to Sea in their *Canoes*" (Defoe, 1719, p. 131). With each new uncertainty, Crusoe exhibits a process of reasoning from minute observations, bringing him incrementally closer to an always-imperfect understanding of what is going on.

Paul Alkon argues that Crusoe only uses probabilistic reasoning to assess events of the past (such as the placement of the footprint), not as a predictive tool to assuage his anxieties about what might happen in the future (Alkon, 1979, pp. 29–62). Yet Jesse Molesworth makes a compelling case that Defoe was perhaps more Bayesian than Alkon acknowledges because "Crusoe the narrator can now look back on his actions as a character as stupid, short-sighted, and motivated by desperation." For Molesworth, the footprint moment demonstrates how "Defoe is … attempting to promote a partnership between statistical probability and narrative probability" (Molesworth, 2010, p. 102). This is a concise description of what I've called the novel of data – the alignment of data and narrative – though I have aimed to show, beyond narrative strategies of representation, how processes of inference work in the novel of data.

Defoe's ways of representing minute particulars – in lists, detailed descriptions, tables, and the like – have been central to scholarly arguments about novelistic realism, and garner much attention; though Defoe's ways of representing methods of reasoning from sense data are the glue that makes empirical knowledge possible. By representing narrative particulars as data or as givens, then providing a detailed focus on the aggregation and integration of particulars and the inferences that bind them together, Defoe encourages his readers to let go of the problems of perception and representation, and focus instead on reasoning our way through matters of uncertainty: faith, providence, trust, and credibility, among others. While this part of the story is certainly not new – especially to scholars of the novel, who are well aware of Defoe's extended efforts to convince readers that Crusoe's is a true story – the mechanism that enables it is counterintuitive. Defoe treats the novel as data not to represent the real, but to suspend it, thus to highlight intellection beyond the point of observation or representation.

3 The Novel of Perception

In the previous section we saw how the function of the novel of data – taking *Robinson Crusoe* as exemplar – is to bracket the problem of perception for the purpose of foregrounding the problem of induction. Defoe foregrounds induction through repetitive and minute descriptions of reasoning under Crusoe's conditions of extreme uncertainty.

The quixotic novel approaches empirical knowledge from the opposite direction. Rather than neutralizing the problem of perception, the quixotic novel puts pressure on perception to demonstrate the difficulty of establishing a sound foundation from which to reason. Whereas Defoe does everything in his power to treat Crusoe's dataset as a given basis for inference – and to treat Crusoe himself as a careful observer and methodical reasoner as he reflects on his circumstances and works his way to conclusions – Charlotte Lennox's *The Female Quixote* (1752) illustrates what happens when its protagonist, Arabella, is in effect trained on an unreliable dataset, seventeenth-century French romance fiction. It's no coincidence that Arabella is a *female* quixote, because the problem of perception was fraught with assumptions about gendered ways of perceiving. If quixotism involves training on unreliable datasets, female quixotism compounds the problem, affording Lennox the opportunity to examine attitudes not only about what women were best positioned to perceive, but also how they perceived it, and how they were perceived perceiving it.

To speak of a novel's protagonist "trained on an unreliable dataset" might seem anachronistic or unpalatable, but this terminology of modern computation reflects a scaled-up version of an old problem of empiricism, which is also the mechanism that enables the satirical and instructive elements of Lennox's novel. How do we manage the fact that our senses respond not simply to what is out there in the world, but also to impressions formed by prior experiences, preferences, and pleasures, which bias subsequent impressions? In *An Essay Concerning Human Understanding*, Locke was concerned that "the feelings of pleasure arising from sensory experience motivated much human thought and action," and "worried that the same feelings of pleasure might make the exercise of reason impossible" (Wragge-Morley, 2020, p. 2). Quixotic figures in the eighteenth-century novel put Locke's concerns to the test.

The Female Quixote is one of many eighteenth-century British novels based on Cervantes's *Don Quixote* (1605–15), and "one of the most sustained discussions of narrative and truth in all of eighteenth-century fiction" (Maioli, 2016, p. 95). Thomas Shelton offered the first English-language translation of *Don Quixote* in 1612 (with a revised edition in 1620), after which point readers of

Figure 5 Don Quixote and Sancho Panza, illustrated by Gustave Doré, 1863

English could obtain iterations of popular translations (including Peter Motteux's in 1700, Charles Jervas's in 1742, Tobias Smollet's in 1755) and more than a handful of novels featuring characters based on Quixote (Hanlon, 2019, pp. 30–40). Like *The Female Quixote*, Richard Graves's *The Spiritual*

Quixote (1774), the anonymously authored *The Amicable Quixote* (1788), and Charles Lucas's *The Infernal Quixote* (1801) announce the influence of Cervantes's novel in the title, though characters including Henry Fielding's Parson Adams in *Joseph Andrews* (which Fielding's title page claims is "Written in Imitation of the Manner of Cervantes, Author of *Don Quixote*") and Tobias Smollett's Launcelot Greaves are also modeled on Quixote. The publication history of eighteenth-century editions of Cervantes's original text, 45 of which appeared in English translation to just 33 in the original Spanish, reflects the immense influence of the Quixote story on the British novel, then eventually the US novel (Wood, 2005, pp. 7–8).

Given this influence – and the extent to which scholars consider *Don Quixote* the primary forerunner of the novel in English – understanding the epistemology of quixotism is essential to understanding the eighteenth-century novel's contributions to empirical knowledge. As Wendy Motooka explains, the epistemological problem quixotic novels illustrate arises from two Lockean views in eighteenth-century Britain, "the first being that reason is universal, and therefore compelling to all rational people . . . the second being that experience and the empirical method are the means through which individuals acquire this universal reason or general view" (Motooka, 1998, p. 2). One of the central functions of quixotic characters in eighteenth-century fiction was to test the limits of empiricism by critically examining the idea that seeing is knowing.

Quixote is an apt character model for interrogating the problem of perception because he possesses two qualities that sit uneasily beside one another. Despite his reputation, he is capable of sound reasoning. Indeed, his ability to make an odd sort of sense is partly what draws other characters into his adventures even as they understand that Quixote is not entirely in his right mind. At the same time, however, Quixote's sense of perception seems off. Or, at least, what he perceives – giants for windmills, or his beloved Dulcinea and her attendants galloping forth on white steeds for three peasant women riding donkeys – is at odds with what most everyone else sees. This combination – the capacity for sound reasoning, even if from fantastical premises, coupled with a perceptive tendency to admit fantastical premises instead of premises based in the physical reality everyone else appears to share – poses important questions for empiricism. Cervantes's character archetype also gave rise to countless travel and adventure plots, since the conflict, humor, suspense, and didactic force of the quixotic novel is so often a function of the quixote seeing and experiencing one thing while everyone else sees and experiences another. The more locales the quixote visits, and the more ranging is the cast of characters with whom the quixote interacts, the greater and more diverse is the sample size by which readers can assess quixotic perception. We find all of these features of *Don Quixote* in abundance in eighteenth-century novels.

But what is the mechanism that enables quixotes to have this experience of the world? The most obvious answer is that quixotes have obsessively read material that does not comport with their external reality and into which they tend to assimilate all of their experiences. From Cervantes's *Don Quixote* to Lennox's *The Female Quixote* and beyond, however, stories of quixotes almost always incorporate realist elements that grant quixotism some degree of empirical plausibility in the physical world of the quixote. This is instrumental to the eighteenth-century rise of the quixotic novel as a vehicle for satirizing large-scale problems, such as social customs and legal and political systems. It is also instrumental to the increasing tendency, over the course of the eighteenth century, for readers to see quixotes as heroes and heroines in failed societies rather than dunces or objects of satire (Paulson, 1998, p. 184). All quixotes, from Miguel de Cervantes's original onward, proceed from an exceptionalist rationale by which they reason deftly from the belief that they are exceptions to everyone else's reality. Thus, for quixotes, the madness in the story belongs not to the quixote, but to everyone else.

The empirical mechanism that grants the quixotic worldview a sneaky plausibility – which makes quixotism an ideal mode for double-edged satire – explains why Henry Fielding wrote, of Arabella, in his 1752 review of Lennox's novel in *The Covent Garden Journal*, "to say the truth, I make no doubt but that most young women of the same vivacity, and of the same innocent good disposition, in the same situation, and with the same studies, would be able to make a large progress in the same follies" (Fielding, 1752). Fielding suggests that a quixotism like Arabella's is a realistic possibility and would be a product not simply of reading material or reading practices, but also of circumstances that interact with impressions from romance reading. Fielding found *The Female Quixote* particularly compelling because he believed that women were more likely than men to perceive faultily, as Arabella does. Lennox critiqued the assumption of faulty female perception by illustrating a world for Arabella in which her external circumstances – those imposed by legal and customary systems that can isolate women and make them dependent on men – fuel her faulty perceptions.

In other words, Lennox's novel made an important empiricist intervention by rejecting the idea of gendered perception, placing the culpability for Arabella's misprision instead on the legal and social customs that force her into a cloistered existence. Rather than relying on notions of innate "female" or "male" perceptive qualities, Lennox puts quixotism to ingenious effect as a mechanism that produces empirically sound but faulty impressions of the world.

As I have argued elsewhere, quixotism produces an empirical feedback loop whereby other characters, either genuinely compelled by or in mockery of the quixote, begin to imitate the quixote's foible or fantasy, and thereby to mirror back to the quixote the very conditions of the fantastical world the quixote envisions (Hanlon, 2019, p. 185). Quixotes do not wholly imagine the world to be other than it is in physical reality; they often receive direct empirical evidence of the world around them appearing or behaving precisely as they would expect from their romance reading. *The Female Quixote* is among the best novels in the period for illustrating this problem. Scott Paul Gordon argues that "for most of *The Female Quixote*, Arabella does not encounter reality at all; she experiences a world of her own making," and consequently Lennox's novel posits that "'reality' can be known only by 'subtracting the conditions of the human mind'" (Gordon, 2006, p. 66). But this isn't quite right. Arabella experiences reality throughout the novel, often reality that appears to fit her quixotic worldview. What throws her off is not an inability to access reality, but a restricted dataset from which to form impressions. We must take into account how the outside world, as it were, also shapes Arabella's experiences and subsequent impressions.

Scholars have rightly regarded *The Female Quixote* as a meditation on the problem of what types of books to read and how (or how not) to read them, particularly in the case of young women, who were assumed less capable than men of tempering the passions with reason and judgment. However, Arabella responds to more than just the textual mediation of French romances in her daily life; she responds to other characters responding to her in the real world of the novel. In other words, Arabella's behavior is not wholly reducible to how and what she reads. A prominent strand of criticism reads Arabella's quixotism as a feminist source of empowerment that enables her to think and act with a degree of self-possession and authority not otherwise available to a woman in her position.[9] Such a reading tacitly relies on the recognition that in Arabella's situation – men controlling the conditions of her inheritance; men attempting to exploit her foible to marry her and take command of her fortune – her quixotism is not only a rational but also an *empirical* response to legal and social scenarios that unjustly constrain her. This is one reason scholars are often disappointed in the novel's ending, in which Arabella accepts Glanville's marriage proposal, and with it the potential to be reined back into patriarchal norms. Of course Arabella misapprehends reality and proceeds with quixotic delusion, but she also reacts to a cast of characters who are almost always trying to deceive her, to play to her quixotism, and to advance their own interests.

---

[9] See, for example, Spacks (1988, pp. 532–542).

Quixotes always have this double edge, this mixture of delusion and piercing insight, so in reading quixotic narratives we should be cautious of questioning quixotic perception and judgment as a default reading. Even when quixotes get things wrong, they also tend to get something right. The problem of perception is at the heart of such quixotic ambivalence.

Arabella's reasoning and behavior are functions of more than obsessive romance reading; they are also functions of her circumstances, thus of a far more complex interaction between two forms of data: literary data from the text and experiential data from the world. Just as Hume considered textual particulars a part of what Porter calls the "databank of literary texts" from which "the laws of both criticism and cognition could be generated inductively," the data that influence Arabella's quixotic behavior are both textual and experiential (Porter, 2018, p. 53). This means that explaining Arabella's behavior requires understanding how the two data sources interact, as opposed the (ironically) quixotic move common in readings of quixotic novels, which is to collapse Arabella's experiences in the world into her experiences of reading (Quixotes even have a tendency to render critics quixotic). Taken simply as satire, the quixotic motif in fiction is fundamentally about obsessive or delusional over-reading of anachronistic or aberrant source material, but the effect of that satirical gesture is produced by a distinct mechanism, the mismatch between what the quixote perceives and what everyone else perceives. To explain even the conventional reading of quixotism as satire, then, requires an explanation of that empirical mechanism on which it rests.

Quixotic empirical breakdown through immersion in compelling fiction was a problem familiar to Royal Society experimentalists in the Baconian tradition. Like Arabella, Robert Boyle was an avid reader of French romances in his youth and was troubled by how effective they were in shaping his thoughts. Boyle, one of the Royal Society fellows most expressly concerned with prose style, would go on to try to reproduce in natural-philosophical writing the compelling literary strategies of the French romances that so arrested him, but for the purpose of moving people closer to empirical knowledge. As Alex Wragge-Morley writes, "the pleasures of rhetoric were to be harnessed, or so Boyle hoped, to the cause of making otherwise unpalatable moral and natural-philosophical discourses as pleasurable as he had once found corrupting romances" (Wragge-Morley, 2020, p. 112).[10]

The idea that words were capable not only of arresting the mind but also of producing sensations more vivid or powerful than pictorial images carried over into the eighteenth century, perhaps best summarized by Joseph Addison's view

---

[10] Here Wragge-Morley draws on work by Principe (1995, pp. 377–397).

that "Words, when well chosen, have so great a Force in them, that a Description often gives us more lively Ideas than the Sight of Things themselves" (Qtd. in Wragge-Morley, 2020, p. 130). Though primarily concerned with matters of conduct – as were so many eighteenth-century novels – *The Female Quixote* suggests that Lennox recognized something about the implications of rhetoric and reading practices for empirical knowledge that Boyle and Addison recognized as well. Clear representation and shared experience of things are not enough for reliable empirical knowledge. Rather, reliable knowledge requires a way of organizing and reasoning from a mixture of data from reading and data from the world, both of which can be vivid, arresting, and compelling. This organizational work is what Locke called the faculty of judgment.

By portraying a challenging dynamic by which data from reading and data from the world interact and mutually influence Arabella's impressions, demanding judgment, Lennox demonstrates a serious complication with the givenness of data. What Arabella learns from seventeenth-century French romances is bad data in the context of her life in eighteenth-century England, yet when other characters respond to Arabella's bizarre behavior, they supply Arabella with real-world data that supports or concords with the bad data of her French romance reading. This in turn reinforces Arabella's divergent behavior. When Arabella is finally cured at the end of the novel, the cure – such as it is – is an epistemological argument about how to distinguish between good and bad data.

Arabella is an heiress to a considerable fortune who nevertheless must marry according to her father's stipulations – which means marrying her cousin, Glanville – to see the entirety of the fortune. Arabella's mother died three days after delivery, leaving Arabella to the care of her nurses, her father, and – most importantly – her late mother's vast library of badly translated seventeenth-century French romances. Arabella's alacritous romance reading produces her quixotic foible, which is to see her lavish but relatively humdrum and isolated country life as a series of romantic adventures, sometimes dangerous.

Among the earliest and most telling examples we get of how Arabella perceives the world is her description of Edward, the gardener. "Unburdening her Mind" to Lucy, the confused but compliant maid who plays Sancho to Arabella's Quixote, Arabella rhapsodizes about what she believes is Edward's juicy secret:

> Ah! she said to her, looking upon *Edward*, who had just passed them, how unfortunate do I think myself in being the Cause of that Passion which makes this illustrious Unknown wear away his Days in so shameful an Obscurity!

Yes, *Lucy*, pursued she, that *Edward*, whom you regard as one of my Father's menial Servants, is a Person of *sublime Quality*, who submits to this Disguise only to have an Opportunity of seeing me every Day (Lennox, 1752, p. 23).

Believing the gardener to be an aristocratic suitor in lowly disguise, toiling for the reward of getting a glimpse of Arabella each day, Arabella perplexes Lucy. To bring Lucy around to her way of seeing things, however, Arabella poses a series of leading questions designed to prompt Lucy to make observations for herself, observations that Arabella expects will bring Lucy's perception in line with hers. That is, though Arabella frequently commands Lucy to participate in quixotic fantasy throughout the novel, she also works to open Lucy's common-sensical mind to the possibility that things are as Arabella sees them, inviting Lucy not simply to take Arabella's word for it (c.f the Royal Society motto, "*nullius in verba*," "on the word of no one," or "take no one's word for it") but to perceive things the way Arabella does:

Has he never unwittingly made any Discovery of himself? Have you not surprised him in Discourse with his faithful 'Squire, who, certainly, lurks hereabouts to recede his Commands, and is haply the Confident of his Passion? Has he never entertained you with any Conversation about me? Or have you never seen any valuable Jewels in his Possession by which you suspected him to be not what he appears? (Lennox, 1752, pp. 23–24).

From one angle, Arabella's questions are unwarranted, as they invite not simply skepticism, but suspicion of Lucy's apprehension of Edward in the absence of cause for such suspicion. From another, however, Arabella's questions begin to unravel an absurd possibility that becomes for Lucy increasingly plausible. In this process of convincing Lucy of something tendentious, Arabella compels Lucy to rely on empirical observation. That is, Lennox portrays Arabella and Lucy arriving together at a shared delusion, but a shared delusion *based in sense data*. Unrealistic as this scenario appears, the fact that Lennox puts sense data at the root of the problem is telling. The possibility that Arabella is correct about Edward and therefore that Lucy is mistaken is grounded in and described in terms of empirical observation. For Lucy replies:

I never took him for for any body else but a simple Gardener; but now you open my Eyes, methinks I can find I have been strangely mistaken; for he does not look like a man of low Degree; and he talks quite in another Manner from our Servants. I never heard him indeed speak of your Ladyship, but once; and that was, when he first saw you walking in the Garden, he asked our *John*, If you was not the Marquis's Daughter? And he said, You was as beautiful as an Angel. As for fine Jewels, I never saw any; and I believe he has none; but he has a Watch, and that looks as if he was something . . . (Lennox, 1752, p. 24).

Lucy's description of the effect of Arabella's line of questioning – "you open my Eyes" – is consistent with Enlightenment metaphors of knowing as seeing and with eighteenth-century empiricist notions of knowledge originating in sense perception (Lakoff and Johnson, 1999, pp. 48–49). Lucy's uneasiness in this moment reflects the credence placed in observational knowledge; she appears unconvinced by Arabella's interpretation of Edward's identity and actions, but at the same time compelled by the recognition that her own observations could be made to align with Arabella's interpretation, despite Lucy's better judgment. "Methinks I can find I have been strangely mistaken" is not the same as "I was mistaken," the latter the kind of pronouncement one makes when wholly convinced of the mistake. Instead, Lucy thinks she "can find" she has been mistaken, which is to say Lucy being mistaken is one of multiple possible outcomes of a shared set of empirical observations between Lucy and Arabella. Because Lucy "can find," based on what she has observed, that she has been mistaken (as opposed to a more definitive "I find I have been mistaken" or "I was mistaken"), she experiences this epistemic limbo – very sensibly – as strange ("methinks I can find I have been strangely mistaken").

Another way of putting this: Lucy can't quite believe her newly opened eyes, though she must entertain belief because – combined with the explanations Arabella supplies from her expectations from romance reading – Lucy's observations really can be made to fit Arabella's impression, however outlandish. As Amelia Dale argues of eighteenth-century quixotic novels, the very trope of "impression," of texts marking or impressing upon readers' minds – particularly "impressionable" young women like Arabella – was one of the ways eighteenth-century readers and critics understood the didactic function (and perils) of novels (Dale, 2019, pp. 1–18). Crucially, for Lucy, being impressed upon by Arabella's view of Edward is partly contingent upon Lucy's own observations. Like Arabella, her "impressions" come not only from what she is told or what she has read, but from what she observes in the world around her. Arabella in turn points Lucy in the direction of Arabella's preferred dataset – those observations that fit together according to Arabella's quixotic worldview – such that Lucy comes to participate not merely in Arabella's delusion, but in Arabella's empiricism.

Once Lucy begins to consider the possibility that her observations of Edward – his appearance not striking her as like "a man of low Degree," that he has in fact inquired after Arabella, and so on – could possibly confirm Arabella's far-fetched belief that Edward is not who he appears to be, each observation colors the next. If, for example, Edward does not look like "a man of low Degree," and although he does not have any fine jewels on his person, he does have a watch, which makes it look "as if he was something." Lucy's thought process in this moment demonstrates how the nature of empirical observation is such that one does not have each sensory experience in isolation or from scratch, as it were, but rather makes observations from the vantage point of having made prior observations and having had prior (and simultaneous experiences). For Arabella and Lucy, observations and experiences compound.

In this way Arabella's line of questioning and pointing out details that technically fit both her far-fetched conclusion about Edward and what Lucy is able to observe with her own eyes begins to make an impression on Lucy that influences her subsequent observations and ideas. Neuroanatomical theories of impressions on the brain, from the mid-seventeenth century onward, sought to explain how sensory experiences could be influenced by memories of prior impressions, revitalized by the imagination. Thomas Willis's *Cerebri Anatome* (1664), for example, advanced the idea that mental images were generated by the transmission of impressions from the outside world via sense perception to the cerebrum, responsible for imagination, and the cortex, responsible for storing memories. Willis believed that particularly strong, vivid, and repeated impressions led to more vivid, longer-lasting memories, a widespread view shared by Hooke, Nehemiah Grew, and other members of the Royal Society, even if they did not all agree with the details of Willis's anatomical explanation for this effect (Wragge-Morley, 2020, p. 152). From this general theory emerged something of a theory of neuroplasticity, wherein it was possible to improve judgment by exposing the brain to the right sensory stimuli, as well as to reduce one's capacity for sound judgment through repeated exposure to "texts written in a poor style – especially a style that corrupted the relationship between words and the things they stood for" (Wragge-Morley, 2020, p. 155). In repetitively reading fantastical French romances in bad translations, Arabella has eroded her faculty of judgment and begins to work likewise on Lucy, such that real-world observations can be assimilated into the quixotic worldview. But we must always bear in mind, as Lennox's novel makes clear, that many of the drivers of Arabella's faulty judgment are circumstantial, and therefore amenable to social change; they are not built-in "female" maladies.

The compounding effect of Lucy's observations also affects Arabella and has in turn a compounding effect on her. This is the empirical feedback loop of quixotic behavior. We do not know whether Arabella's belief that Edward is not who he seems comes in any part from Arabella's empirical observation (of the sort Lucy reports), but when Lucy tells Arabella that by her observations there might be something to Arabella's view – indeed, that Lucy now believes herself "strangely mistaken" – she externally validates Arabella's view. Arabella now sees Lucy assenting to Arabella's impression of Edward and bolstering it with observations about Edward's appearance, manner of speaking, watch, and so on.

Whereas the conventional understanding of quixotic behavior is that Arabella is delusional, her impression of Edward wholly contrived, fantastical, and based entirely in romance reading, such an understanding fails to account for a central feature of such moments of quixotic delusion. Namely, that even the faulty judgments of Arabella – and then Lucy – are empirically grounded. This is what I mean when I suggest *The Female Quixote* puts pressure on the problem of perception to expose the difficulty of deriving empirical knowledge from sense data, a difficulty recognized by Locke, Boyle, Hooke, and later Berkeley and Hume. Lennox makes use of the quixote motif not simply to theorize the problem of perception and the Lockean principle of nonresemblance between ideas in the mind and things in the world, but to put that principle on display through Arabella's engagements with real-world characters and surroundings.

The brief exchange between Arabella and Lucy over Edward is not anomalous in Lennox's novel; it is the very sort of comical but, as Lucy experiences it, "strangely" compelling portrayal of fraught empiricism that defines Lennox's epistemological intervention in *The Female Quixote*. As Roger Maioli observes, "Lennox has made sure that the world of romance resembles the world of Arabella's experience" (Maioli, 2016, p. 100). As a consequence, Arabella is almost always able to find (recall Lucy's "methinks I can find . . . ") an empirical analogue in the world of the expectations she has cultivated in romance reading. When Fielding imagined in his review of *The Female Quixote* that, given a set of circumstances like those of Arabella, there might be real-life Arabellas sporadically located along the English countryside, he implicitly acknowledged not only the influence of quixotic reading practices to impress upon minds, nor simply the pitfalls of being impressionable, but also the fact that when real life looks like fantasy, empirical knowledge is a function of judgment and sound inference, not simply observation and representation.

We witness the difficulty of the problem of perception in one of the more violent (and dangerous) moments in *The Female Quixote*, when Glanville and Hervey, two of Arabella's suitors, come to blows over her. The situation develops innocently enough, as Hervey views from afar an exchange between Arabella and Glanville that ends with Arabella galloping off. Because Arabella had previously dismissed and confounded Hervey, he figures Glanville has just suffered the same exasperating treatment, so approaches him, laughing and sympathetic. But in seeking sympathy with Glanville, and inquiring whether he is "not disturbed at the ridiculous Folly of a Lady I saw you with just now . . . fit for a Mad-house," he gravely offends Glanville, who is not only a genuine suitor of Arabella, favored to marry her but also her cousin. Thus offended by the liberties Hervey has taken in speaking that way of Arabella, Glanville retorts – "being in very ill Humour," because in fact he *was* just frustrated by Arabella's behavior – that it was "very impertinent to speak of a Lady of her Quality and Merit so rudely." Hervey finds Glanville's quick temper not only humorous but also, in a moment of incisive reading, comically reflective of Arabella's own chivalric modes of courtship and address, as if Glanville has been impressed upon by Arabella's quixotism. Indeed, he has! But as Glanville, further offended at being laughed at, strikes Hervey with the blunt end of his whip, and Hervey draws his sword and shoves Glanville back, and Glanville draws his sword to square up with Hervey, it becomes clear that Hervey, too, has been unwittingly drawn into the very romance plot he was mocking (Lennox, 1752, pp. 156–157).

As the two men fight, Arabella, "who had not rid far, concealing herself behind some Trees, saw all the Actions of her Lover, and intended Ravisher; and, being possessed with an Opinion of her Cousin's Cowardice, was extremely rejoiced to see him fall upon his Enemy first, and with so much Fury" (Lennox, 1752, p. 157). Once again Arabella's empirically observable life confirms her quixotic expectations. And Arabella is not the only one compelled to behave as if reenacting a romance plot. Whereas she sees the fight between Glanville and Hervey as an instance of Glanville defending her honor – honor, firstly, in the bodily sense of forestalling a perceived "Ravisher" come to seize Arabella and carry her off for illicit ends – the men are really fighting because Hervey offended Glanville's honor, in a second sense, his pride. At the same time, however, Glanville's retort to Hervey was indeed about defending Arabella's honor in a third sense – her reputation – which was also the reason for the fight. All of these forms of honor are interrelated and rooted in chivalry, even as their manifestations have changed by the eighteenth century. Though Arabella, watching from afar, holds a literal view of the romance plot unfolding before her eyes (Glanville is rescuing her from a "Ravisher"), Glanville's actions are still broadly chivalric, which is to say motivated by surviving manifestations of chivalric code. Likewise, both Glanville and Hervey are real suitors, the former out of rapidly intensifying affection for Arabella even as she continues to frustrate him, the latter out of interest in her inheritance.

As in the example of Edward the gardener, in which Lucy's assent to Arabella's interpretation of Edward lends external and empirical credence to Arabella's view, the fight between Glanville and Hervey empirically comports with Arabella's belief that the surrounding world functions like a seventeenth-century French romance plot. Even as Arabella's view of things is based in misconception, the conclusion that much of her life aligns with the expectations she draws from romance reading is not unreasonable. She has multiple suitors who quarrel over her – sometimes by drawing weapons – and compete for her affection; she lives a removed and cloistered life in the countryside; she is regularly exoticized and commands the attention of strangers who accost her for attention in various ways (as when she visits Bath), if not always for the reasons she suspects. In portraying Arabella and her surroundings this way, Lennox's novel directly addresses the problem of perception, isolating its fraught nature by demonstrating at length how common sensory experiences among different characters can produce radically different understandings of what is happening.

The Female Quixote's ending underscores how Lennox queries the problem of perception through quixotic vignettes of common observations and mismatched interpretations. The ending has attracted much scholarly attention and discussion, the bulk of which concerns its implications for the novel's feminist critique. As in Don Quixote's deathbed confession, quixotic figures in eighteenth-century novels frequently encounter a conversion moment in which either their quixotism persists (Parson Adams doing his best to maintain his antiquated clerical solemnity in celebrating the marriage of Joseph and Fanny) or in which the quixote is converted away from quixotism and made to see the error of their ways. *The Female Quixote* is the latter sort. Arabella sits down with the Doctor, a Samuel Johnson type, and through conversation with the Doctor is at last prevailed upon to renounce quixotism and marry Glanville with a vow that she will "endeavour to make [herself] as worthy as [she is] able of such a favourable Distinction" of being the "Partner for Life" of such a "Man of … Sense and Honour" (Lennox, 1752, p. 383).[11] From the standpoint of feminist critique, this is a disappointing moment, because the quixotism Arabella renounces has frequently empowered her throughout the novel in scenarios in which women typically would not have commanded such authority. Eve Tavor Bannet argues, for example, that "in making Arabella a Dulcinea, Lennox transformed the latter from a figure who was, in her way, as much a passive occasion for masculine heroics as [Henry Fielding's] Fanny [in *Joseph Andrews*], into a controlling agent" (Bannet, 2007, p. 562). Yet the implications of Arabella's conversion moment for Lennox's foregrounding of the problem of perception remain underdeveloped.

Roger Maioli's brief study of Lennox's ending remains the most thorough account of its epistemological implications. For Maioli, the penultimate chapter of *The Female Quixote*, in which the Doctor reasons Arabella out of quixotism, resembles the Johnsonian argument that the role of the novel – as opposed to the romance – is to "align the passions with the cause of virtue," or to offer representations that depart from reality by portraying characters and scenes

---

[11] Though there is not sufficient evidence to confirm it, scholars have suspected that Johnson may have written the concluding episode of *The Female Quixote* featuring the Doctor, on grounds that the Doctor's views closely align with those of Johnson, who was a supporter of Lennox's work. For a discussion of this, see Spacks (1990, pp. 14–16).

more virtuous than reality. Although it resembles this Johnsonian argument, per Maioli, the conversation between the Doctor and Arabella is perhaps more concerned than was Johnson with perceptual difficulty and the problems it poses for reliable knowledge (in the case of *The Female Quixote*, reliable knowledge of the social world). That is, Maioli is correct that Lennox had Johnsonian didactic aims, but it is the epistemic question at the heart of *The Female Quixote* that makes its didacticism possible.

"For most of their debate," writes Maioli, "Arabella and the Doctor are evaluating romance on a different scale, one in which factual truth matters" (Maioli, 2016, p. 98). We can observe Lennox's interest in truth in the novel, well in excess of Johnson's, when the Doctor tells Arabella, referring to Samuel Richardson's *Clarissa* (1748), that "truth is not always injured by fiction" (Lennox, 1752, p. 377). Bender calls this moment "a ringing endorsement of the newly defined novel of experience" (Bender, 2012, p. 24). Nevertheless, in Maioli's reading, while *The Female Quixote* "operat[es] within the framework of empiricism" by depicting with some degree of accuracy "the domestic consequences of patriarchal norms," it ultimately does not attempt to "harmonize empiricism with a propositional defense of novels," or resolve the philosophical challenges to empirical knowledge in the novel raised in Arabella and the Doctor's exchange (Maioli, 2016, pp. 105–106).

However, to understand what's happening here, it's important to address an orthogonal matter in the conclusion of *The Female Quixote*: not the question of whether Lennox offers a defense of propositional knowledge in the novel through accurate representation, but instead how Lennox's ending handles the problem of perception. That is, Lennox's epistemology of the novel is more like the novel *as* epistemology, a novelistic interrogation of the reliability of sense perception as a basis for knowing. Even if the conclusion is that, following Arabella's impressions and eventual conversion from quixotism, we have cause to view empirical observation as a gateway to knowledge with some ambivalence, this is nevertheless a contribution to eighteenth-century empiricist discussions of the problem of perception. Again, rather than theorizing the problem, as did Locke, Berkeley, and Hume, Lennox used the quixotic motif to illustrate and draw out the problem, to push empiricism to its logical limits. As I have shown, one way to do that is to highlight, as Lennox does, the perceptual problems that arise when modern, eighteenth-century women are treated (legally, customarily) in so many ways that actually resemble antiquated chivalric romance. That is, how fantastical can an interpretation of reality be while remaining grounded in sense data, particularly when social circumstances afford such a limited dataset?

Arabella requires the Doctor to make his case against her quixotism by demonstrating three propositions: that the romances or "histories" Arabella reads are (1) fictional, (2) absurd, and (3) criminally dangerous (Lennox, 1752, p. 374). As Maioli rightly notes, the Doctor struggles mightily to prove the first to Arabella, whose empirical experience often justifies her behavior, however outlandish (Maioli, 2016, p. 99). Arabella believes the romance fiction she reads is nonfiction, and casts doubt on the idea that fiction could mirror reality, such that her defense of what she reads is not based on its fictional correspondence to reality – its verisimilitude – but on the belief that it is an historical account of reality (Maioli, 2016, p. 100). The extent to which the Doctor struggles to demonstrate that Arabella is wrong on this point is a reflection of Lennox's skill in working with a quixotic protagonist and constructing scenarios in which empirical observation and quixotic perception are reconcilable. Indeed, even when the Doctor finally convinces Arabella that her romances are fictional, he does so not by refuting Arabella's empirical justification for believing what she does, but by asserting that she takes his word for it because she is not very experienced: "You have yet had little Opportunity of knowing the Ways of Mankind" (Lennox, 1752, p. 379). At this moment Lennox finally employs a principle of the novel of data, akin to Defoe's strategy in *Robinson Crusoe*; the Doctor premises reliability not on empirical observation as such, but on the aggregation of many observations, some of which might be in error, but all of which, together, should lead to a fairly reliable picture of the world. What Arabella ultimately finds compelling about this line of reasoning is not that she is wrong about what she has perceived, but that she may not have done enough perceiving at this point in her life to have a representative picture of the whole.

Arabella's acceptance of this line of argument echoes, in its seeming implausibility, Crusoe's conversion of Friday to Christianity, a conversation in which Crusoe struggles to answer the substance of Friday's probing questions about Crusoe's beliefs, yet mysteriously prevails upon Friday's conscience anyway. In principle, the Doctor has not demonstrated point (1), which is required to demonstrate point (2) about the absurdity of Arabella's romances. The Doctor prevails upon Arabella ultimately by moving from an unproven assertion about point (1) (in effect, "trust me, I know more about the world than you do, so what looks to you like reality is actually fiction") to anchor point (2) – because Arabella is convinced by the principle that more sense data is more likely to lead to more accurate or less absurd conclusions – then to make point (3) by demonstrating a principle that is less about empiricism than about the Johnsonian and Richardsonian arguments that fiction should set a *moral* example. Arabella realizes that, truth value aside, what she reads spurs her to impetuous and dangerous acts, so abandons quixotism: "my Heart yields to the Force of Truth, and I now wonder how the Blaze of Enthusiastic Bravery, could hinder me from remarking with Abhorrence the Crime of deliberate unnecessary Bloodshed" (Lennox, 1752, p. 381). By this point in the argument, the novel has moved on from the core epistemic questions addressed in points (1) and (2).

The fact that Lennox switches tracks in the end from matters of epistemic concern to matters of moral concern should not discourage us from investigating *The Female Quixote*'s engagement with empiricist philosophy in the period, particularly the problem of perception. As I have suggested, Locke was ambivalent about the basis of sensitive knowledge. Although empiricists of the period typically used the language of immediacy – "immediately perceived," "immediate object of perception" – to suggest the closest possible proximity, or the narrowest possible gap, between the physical object perceived and the sensation of it, they were also aware of Locke's principle of nonresemblance between ideas and things, thus the fraught nature of perception. This is important for the third part of Locke's three-part theory of perception, the part that Lennox takes up most explicitly in *The Female Quixote*: (1) the body's sensory apparatus is stimulated by a thing in the world; (2) the stimulation conveys information to the brain via the nerves; (3) the brain produces an idea in the mind (Dicker, 2019, p. 263).

The inferences required to get from part (1) to part (3) create an epistemic problem with which Locke intensely grappled, which Georges Dicker calls "the argument from the multiple alternative causes of any perceptual experience." The basis of this argument, which Descartes flagged in the *Sixth Meditation*, is that we can have perceptual experiences without having been stimulated by the physical thing we perceive. If therefore we cannot know whether it was a physical thing that set in motion parts (1) to (3), then "no physical thing is ever immediately perceived" (Dicker, 2019, pp. 265–266). This aspect of the problem of perception for Locke means not that the physical world is unknowable, but that it is not knowable solely on the basis of a perceptual experience (Dicker, 2019, pp. 269–270). This is how the novel of perception – of which *The Female Quixote* is a prominent example – approaches empirical knowledge from the opposite direction of the novel of data. If the novel of data isolates the problem of induction by neutralizing the problem of perception, the novel of perception demonstrates the importance of judgment and inductive reasoning by isolating the fraught nature of perception. In this way, Lennox's novel functions like an experimental test of the perceptual component of empiricism. Lennox need not force a result in this experiment by arguing away the problem of perception in Descartes, Locke, and Hume to make a significant contribution to eighteenth-century epistemology, or to model with clarity the problem of knowing from sense perception.

Hume's attitude toward the novel as an experimental technology was largely skeptical, even as Hume relied on thought experiments or structured fictional accounts in his own work (Maioli, 2016, pp. 41–42). Bender, however, views Hume's project of "experiments . . . from a cautious observation of human life" as compatible with those of the novel, and this view of the novel's epistemic function also works well as a description of the kind of caution Lennox supplies in *The Female Quixote* (Qtd. in Bender, 2012, p. 27). Even if Hume was not keen on novels as vehicles for propositional knowledge, nor Locke, Berkeley, and Hume capable of resolving the problem of perception, Lennox marshaled quixotism toward a form of inquiry well in line with what empiricist philosophers were working on by the mid-eighteenth century.

Lennox's core contribution to empiricist thought in *The Female Quixote* was also an expressly feminist contribution, but not in the way scholars tend to think. It's not just that Arabella's quixotism gives her agency, nor that it illustrates a particularly "female" way of perceiving against a masculine empirical norm. Rather, the quixotic-empirical feedback loop Lennox employs allows her to show how the legal and customary restriction of women's opportunities for experience, observation, and reasoning in the world leads to perceptual problems and problems of judgment. In the end, this is not only a feminist problem bearing on women's rights and education in ways that Mary Wollstonecraft would take up later in the century, but also an epistemological problem, a problem for any theory of empiricism. The principles of social epistemology that underwrite the view that the more – and the more diverse – the observers, the more accurate and reliable are the conclusions they're likely to reach, are underdeveloped in the empiricist philosophies of Locke, Berkeley, and Hume, but prominent in *The Female Quixote*. The following section examines how the principles of social epistemology work in novels of testimony.

4 The Novel of Testimony

The novel of testimony – of which Frances Burney's *Evelina* (1778) is exemplary – incorporates elements of the novel of data and the novel of perception, synthesizing these into practical issues of testimony and judgment. Like embedded lists and charts in the novel of data, *Evelina*'s letters function like evidentiary accounts and provide multiple perspectives on the same unfolding story. As Melissa Pino suggests, "Burney's goal for *Evelina* was a realistic depiction of her characters"; however, "such 'sober Probability' indicates a method in which general observations can be made only after a close examination of a range of empirical evidence; this method does not attempt to make disparate realities conform to a pre-determined paradigm" (Pino, 2010, p. 278). Like the novel of perception, the multiplicity of first-person accounts in *Evelina* undercut the absolute authority of any single account, encouraging readers to form judgments based on a survey of all available evidence. The novel of testimony – Samuel Richardson's *Pamela* (1740), Burney's *Evelina* (1778), and Jane Austen's *Sense and Sensibility* (1811) form a representative cluster – generates concern by portraying vulnerable protagonists, often women, in high-stakes social scenarios, putting pressure on matters of judgment because their fate depends on it, and linking sound judgment to the ability to discern reliable from unreliable testimony.[12] In so doing, the novel of testimony makes judges of readers, inviting them to weigh the credibility of accounts. In what follows we can see how *Evelina* broke with *Pamela* and pointed the novel of testimony in the direction of credibility, a major contribution to social epistemology in the period that would set the stage – in this respect – for the novels of Jane Austen.

    Much social judgment in *Evelina* – both within the world of the novel and in the novel's invitation to readers to decide whether to trust the judgments of a female protagonist Burney tells us in the preface is "young, artless, and inexperienced" – is rooted in Burney's portrayal of the credibility of written testimony (Burney, 1778, p. 10). Stephanie Insley Hershinow observes that Samuel Johnson thought Burney's "particular gift was to conjure an illusion of experience from its absence." In Johnson's words, "'Evelina' seems a work that should result from long experience, and deep and intimate knowledge of the world; yet it has been written without either" (Hershinow, 2019, pp. 113–114). *Evelina* operates from the basis of this paradox of portrayals of naiveté and of sound judgment; in Pino's words, "Evelina employs an innate capacity for judgment, independent of experience, to come to her conclusions" (Pino, 2010, p. 278). *Evelina* focuses on issues of credibility by giving readers a protagonist who lacks experience but excels at observation and social judgment, which fuels its satirical portrayal of London society.

    As Pino observes, Burney's novels have been subject to frequent "negative readings – negative in that they foreground or emphasize what Burney did not or could not do," even in "criticism that operates on the premise that her work is worth the while." When Pino, who reads *Evelina* as deeply and satirically

---

[12] Since I invoke *Sense and Sensibility* as an example of the novel of judgment alongside two epistolary novels, I note that Austen initially wrote the *Sense and Sensibility* in the 1790s, as an epistolary novel called *Elinor and Marianne*, before later reworking and updating it for Regency tastes. Austen's free indirect style would achieve many of the epistemic affordances of the discarded epistolary form. See Doody (1997, p. 86).

engaged with eighteenth-century philosophy of aesthetics, suggests that Burney's critics view the idea "that Burney could respond intelligently to a complex of ideas whose contributors include Burke, Locke, and Hume" as "too much of a stretch," she identifies a considerable omission in studies of *Evelina*. Burney's novel evinces her awareness of hot-button philosophical topics of the period in which she wrote (Pino, 2010, pp. 266–267).[13]

Intertwined with matters of judgment and testimony are matters of credibility. As historians and philosophers of science have shown, from Shapin and Schaffer's concept of virtual witnessing to Helen Longino's concept of "transformative interrogation" to Naomi Oreskes's defense of scientific knowledge in the aggregate, the establishment of matters of fact and the generation of explanatory knowledge is a social process frequently dependent on contested observations and communication within and between epistemic communities.[14] Longino's concept of transformative interrogation, "the collective give-and-take of critical discussion" within a scientific community, bringing multiple perspectives to bear on the question, is especially useful for understanding how novels can model the process of knowledge production (Longino, 1990, p. 79). The abundance of eighteenth-century novels that focused on social systems and social judgments is a valuable and unfortunately neglected archive for those interested in social epistemology.

Surveying the sociology of social and natural science, Steven Shapin writes "the study of credibility ... became simply coextensive with the study of knowledge, including scientific knowledge. In sociological terms of art, an individual's *belief* (or an individual's claim) was contrasted to collectively held *knowledge*. The individual's belief did not become collective – and so part of knowledge – until or unless it had won credibility" (Shapin, 1995, p. 257). An important principle of Shapin's observation that the study of knowledge production is coextensive with the study of credibility is that "if we say that scientific claims have always got to win credibility, then that makes them like the claims of ordinary life" (Shapin, 1995, p. 257). Scholars have noted the centrality of that phrase, "ordinary life," to the eighteenth-century novel. As Burney puts it in the preface to *Evelina*, "to draw characters from nature, though not from life, and to mark the manners of the times, is the attempted plan of the following letters" (Burney, 1778, p. 9). For Shapin, the fact that the study of credibility is a matter not strictly of scientific claims but also of the claims of ordinary life "means that we can make use of many of the resources and procedures that feature in academic inquiries about other

---

[13] Pino focuses on aesthetics in *Evelina*, but also points out that eighteenth-century aesthetics heavily relied on empirical accounts of the aesthetic experience.

[14] See Longino (1990) and Oreskes (2019).

practices" (Shapin, 1995, p. 259). Further, "there is no limit to the consider-ations that might be relevant to securing credibility, and, therefore, no limit to the considerations which the analyst of science might give attention" (Shapin, 1995, p. 260). Examining how novels portray what Shapin calls the "credit-economy" of knowledge is an important component of epistemological inquiry (Shapin, 1995, p. 258).

As an epistolary novel, *Evelina* affords the ability to represent multiple and sometimes conflicting character points of view on a common subject or obser-vation. In this way the epistolary novel models a version of Longino's trans-formative interrogation by offering readers a bird's-eye view of characters' disputed accounts and subjective attachments. Sociologists of science generally believe that it is very difficult to study a knowledge dispute or controversy once it has been resolved, so tend to emphasize the study of "science in action" to gain an understanding of how disputes play out. By contrast, historians of science attempt to reconstruct past controversies to gain a similar kind of insight (Schaffer, 2020). The epistolary novel provides a model through which we can track character judgment and disputation, the evidence available to characters, the ways they reason, the motivations they bring to an observation or judgment, and their credibility as observers or claimants. Even epistolary novels, such as *Pamela* or *Evelina*, dominated by one correspondent who observes others, can foreground the collective assembly of knowledge by highlighting communica-tion and interpretation among characters. Even as Evelina's correspondences occupy the vast majority of Burney's novel, Burney furnishes readers with crucial moments of triangulation.

The eighteenth-century novel of testimony was adept at examining the interaction of testimony and credibility. The publication of *Pamela* famously called into question the reliability of testimony as a basis for judgment. What William Warner calls the "Pamela Media Event," which had "long-term conse-quences for novel reading in Britain," became an "ambient, pervasive phenom-enon which properly compel[led] the attention and opinions of those with a modicum of 'curiosity'" (Warner, 1998, pp. 177–178). As scholars of shown, central to the Pamela media event was the intrigue of the visual as a way of knowing and trusting. Kristina Straub notes that *Pamela* "has been accused of appealing to its audience's voyeurism" (Straub, 1989, p. 419). Bethany Wong observes the theatrical elements of how we evaluate and discuss Pamela's credibility, implicitly invoking the role of the visual – and the rhetoric of the visual – in a convincing performance. "Although many contemporary readers were persuaded by Pamela's disinterested integrity and lauded her example," writes Wong, "Antipamelist detractors cast the heroine's character flaws along theatrical lines." Wong notes that in Henry Fielding's *Shamela*

(1741), Shamela's mother "sold Oranges in the Play-House," and in Eliza Haywood's *Anti-Pamela; or, Feign'd Innocence Detected* (1741), Syrena Tricksey took up acting during childhood. In both cases, Wong observes, elements of the theatrical take on sexual valences with further implications for how readers understood their character and credibility (Wong, 2016, p. 180). Another foundational text in the anti-Pamela tradition, Haywood's *Anti-Pamela; or, Feign'd Innocence Detected*, likewise responds to questions of credible testimony in Richardson's novel, particularly as concerns visual observation. As Rivka Swenson notes, one of the contexts *Anti-Pamela* responds to is "the contemporary fascination with the dynamics of vision as a physical as well as social process . . . the narrator advises readers to draw an 'Observation' from Haywood's own 'look into the[ir] World'" (Swenson, 2010, p. 27). I only add, by way of synthesis, that from *Pamela* to *Shamela* and *Anti-Pamela*, the narrative strategy of inviting voyeurism establishes visuality and witnessing as grounds for judgments of credibility, which means judgments of performance become judgments of credibility.

As these scholars have demonstrated, much of the Pamela / anti-Pamela controversy was over testimonial credibility and to what extent Richardson modeled it compellingly in *Pamela*. Consider, for example, one of the most poignantly satirical moments in Henry Fielding's parody of *Pamela, Shamela*. As Shamela lies in bed with Mrs. Jervis, Booby enters the room and insinuates himself in the bed between the two women, who pretend to be asleep. "I hear him just coming in at the Door," Shamela narrates. "You see I write in the present Tense . . . Well, he is in Bed between us, we both shamming a Sleep, he steals his Hand into my Bosom, which I, as if in my Sleep, press close to me with mine, and then pretend to awake" (Fielding, 1741, p. 318). Fielding's parody hits the mark not only by rendering the salaciousness of *Pamela* hyperbolic ("he steels his Hand into my Bosom") and the piousness of Pamela dubious but also by playing with the plausibility of written testimony and its proximity to the real. "You see I write in the present Tense" calls attention to the way Pamela's letters can seem a little too narrated, as if contrived and fabricated rather than credibly related after the fact. The image of Shamela scribbling in the dark in the precise moment when Booby throws himself upon her and Mrs. Jarvis, on the other side of Booby, pretends to sleep is quintessential burlesque and certainly works on that register, but it also satirizes a contrived rhetoric of the immediacy of experience and of relation, and in turn the credibility of the account. The reason the "immediately perceived" is meant to bracket the problem of perception in novel of data – to render presumptive or provisional the reliability of sense data – is also what makes Fielding's burlesque scene work. By rendering absurd

Shamela's claim to the immediacy of the written account, expressed in visual terms – "You see I write in the present Tense" – Fielding illuminates the problem with taking the epistolary form as immediate, trustworthy testimony. If *Pamela* called into question the reliability of testimony as a basis for judgment, *Evelina* demonstrated what skilled judgment could look like, even for a character who – like her author – is frequently portrayed as inexperienced and naive. In both novels, the epistolary form plays a significant role in foregrounding judgments about the reliability and credibility of testimony, because letters in the voices of multiple characters frequently reveal multiple perspectives on the same observation or scenario. From this form of presentation, readers can triangulate their understanding of what is happening and whose testimony is reliable or unreliable, as the case may be. In *The Female Quixote*, Lennox uses quixotism to enact a reductio ad absurdum of perceptual knowledge, using the quixotic motif to portray scenarios in which Arabella struggles to evaluate and norm a combination of textual and sense data. The epistolary novel of testimony offers just such a norming device in the multiple perspectives of the epistolary form itself.

Embedding the narrative in the form of a letter presents the narrative account as if an original, primary-source document. As Peter DeGabriele writes, "the letter in *Evelina* is part of the material world of sense, and is not merely a narrative mechanism for producing psychological interiority" (DeGabriele, 2014, p. 23). DeGabriele suggests the epistolary form in *Evelina* is like the concept of legal fiction, "a mechanism of the law by which particular and material circumstances are brought within the purview of the law through an arbitrary formal subsumption of those circumstances within the terms of legal discourse" (DeGabriele, 2014, p. 24). In the preface to *Evelina*, Burney affirms this notion of the presentation of letters as evidence from which to reason and judge, announcing that "the following letters are presented to the public," offered up for scrutiny. Similar to Defoe's strategy in the novel of data, Burney uses the epistolary form to close the epistemic gap between the account and the reader, giving the impression of the materiality and immediacy of documentary evidence, but – unlike Defoe – triangulating readers' judgments by presenting multiple points of view on the same set of affairs. In this sense, the letters resemble artifacts, a type of object that, as Crystal Lake incisively points out, was tied to the seventeenth-century archaeological notion of things "speaking for themselves" (Lake, 2020, p. 4). But together they form a kind of data. And the credibility of their speech, as it were, is a function of how we judge their authors.

Beyond the use of the epistolary form to give the impression of immediacy in judgments of the credibility of accounts, Burney conceives of knowledge in

Evelina as a particularly social phenomenon, requiring scrutiny of testimony. Indeed, the sociality of novel reading – including all its potential pitfalls – is the foundation of Burney's defense of the novel in the preface. Crucially, just as Lennox's philosophical intervention significantly relied on rendering the quixote female, Burney's preface is primarily addressed to female readers of novels, for whom Burney imagines novel reading is especially perilous territory, a source of feminine "distemper." As Burney writes:

> Perhaps were it possible to effect the total extirpation of novels, our young ladies in general, and boarding-school damsels in particular, might profit from their annihilation: but since the distemper they have spread seems incurable, since their octagon bids defiance to the medicine of advice or reprehension, and since they are found to baffle all the mental art of physic, save what is prescribed by the slow regimen of Time, and bitter diet of Experience, surely all attempts to contribute other number of those which may be read, if not with advantage, at lest without injury, ought rather to be encouraged than condemned. (Burney, 1778, pp. 9–10)

If novels are a social contagion, reasons Burney, capable of misleading young women to the extent that it would be advantageous yet impossible to get rid of *all novels*, the cure turns out to be more novels of a better sort. Here Burney's comments lend credence to the idea that the novel and the romance were not well enough understood as distinct genres, since Burney includes among "Novelists" not only Henry Fielding, Samuel Richardson, and Tobias Smollett, but also Samuel Johnson, who authored the "oriental tale" *Rasselas* (1759), Jean-Jacques Rousseau, who authored *Julie* (1761) and *Emile* (1762), and Pierre Marivaux, who authored the unfinished romance novels *La Vie de Marianne* (1731–41) and *Le Paysan Parvenu* (1734–35) (Burney, 1778, p. 9). Burney's footnote in the preface offers something of a tongue-in-cheek apology for "rank[ing] the authors of Rasselas and Eloise as Novelists." In this sense, bearing in mind that Burney explicitly invokes the romance genre in the preface as if part of the novel genre, "the novel" includes both stories that comport with "Nature" and stories of a more fantastical sort, the former which can be read "with advantage," or "at least without injury," while the latter are justifiably condemnable. To read a novel – whether "Natural" or fantastical – is for Burney, as for many other theorists of and commentators on the novel in the eighteenth century, to be socialized in some way. In turn the ways novels function or malfunction in socializing readers epistemically is a social problem or social benefit, as the case may be (Burney, 1778, p. 9).

It's worth noting that Burney's preface is composed in a wry tone, not unlike Fielding's preface to *Joseph Andrews*. The preface is full of hyperbolic apology for "the humble Novelist" and performative humility, yet also like Fielding's preface it contains a theory of the novel (Burney, 1778, p. 9). Following her division between the types of novels one might read to advantage versus types that might mislead readers, Burney's theory of the novel addresses the question of novelistic verisimilitude, somewhat conventionally, as probabilistic representation. Burney discusses the "Romance" as a negative example through which to frame her offering in *Evelina*:

> Let me, therefore, prepare for disappointment those who, in the perusal of these sheets, entertain the gentle expectation of being transported to the fantastic regions of Romance, where Fiction is colored by all the gay tints of luxurious Imagination, where Reason is an outcast, and where the sublimity of the Marvellous rejects all aid from sober Probability. The heroine of these memoirs, young, artless, and inexperienced, is "No faultless Monster, that the World ne'er saw," but the offspring of Nature, and of Nature in her simplest attire. (Burney, 1778, p. 10)

There's hyperbole in the description of romance as "colored by all the gay tints of luxurious Imagination," rendering reason an "outcast," but the view holds that there is something laudatory about avoiding imaginative overindulgence in fiction. Burney's invocation of the virtues of probability and simplicity in a fictional account, together with her prior claim that *Evelina* will draw "characters from nature, though not from life," is an endorsement of novelistic verisimilitude as probable representation. For Burney, the novel should not conflate fiction with what today we would call an historical account, but should model probable worlds. Positioning herself in relation to Rousseau, Richardson, Henry Fielding, and Smollett, Burney seeks a different path to avoid creating an inferior copy of a prevalent, empiricist model of the novel:

> To avoid what is common, without adopting what is unnatural, must limit the ambition of the vulgar herd of authors; however zealous, therefore, my veneration of gate great writers I have mentioned, however I may feel myself enlightened by the knowledge of Johnson, charmed with the eloquence of Rousseau, softened by the pathetic powers of Richardson, and exhilarated by the wit of Fielding, and humor of Smollet; I yet presume not to attempt pursuing the same ground which they have tracked; whence, though they may have cleared the weeds, they have also culled the flowers, and though they have rendered the path plain, they have left it barren (Burney, 1778, p. 10).

In this justification for what follows in *Evelina* we can observe both a respectful rejection of taking prior, prominent novelistic fiction as models and a more directly evaluative claim about such models. Writers of early- and mid-eighteenth-century novels "cleared the weeds" but also "culled the flowers" and left a "barren" field. The novel of data seemed, in retrospect, impractical for the demands of daily life and the social pressures facing young women in particular, and this is where Burney's novelistic strategy departs from that of Richardson, among others. Given Burney's stated admiration for fiction that verges into the territory of romance alongside the oft-referenced staples of the early-eighteenth-century novel (Fielding, Richardson, Smollett), we have reason to believe Burney's "cleared the weeds but culled the flowers" judgment is to do with overzealous policing of the amorous and imaginative components of novels. That is, though imagination was widely considered in the eighteenth century "the *source* of sexual feeling," and thus something to be wary of for a writer in Burney's position who aimed to convey to critics a sense of concern for propriety, it is also a source of moral modeling (Spacks, 1974, p. 38). Burney's Johnsonian interest in writing novels that can be read, in her words, "if not with advantage, at least without injury" means imagining probable scenarios that do not imitate life as such, but portray ways of navigating social difficulties in moral and respectable ways. Whereas, like Richardson in *Pamela*, Burney was interested in the novel as a vehicle for moral instruction, what Burney understood (that Richardson failed to understand) is that credibility is as essential to moral as to empirical judgment. In this way in particular Burney's *Evelina* functioned as a work of social epistemology with a convincing grasp of the value of probabilistic thinking for moral instruction.

We find support for this probabilistic theory of the novel in Burney's journals, as well as in her last novel, *The Wanderer* (1814). In 1768, for example, she wrote of the fictional letters in Elizabeth Rowe's epistolary *Friendship and Death* (1728) "they are so very enthusiastick, that the religion she preaches rather disgust and & cloys than charms & elevates – & so romantick, that every word betrays improbability, instead of disguising fiction, & displays the Author, instead of human nature" (Crump, 2002, p. 55). Likewise, in the prefatory material to *The Wanderer*, Burney writes that a novel should convey "useful precepts" and that it "is, or ought to be, a picture of supposed, but natural and probable human existence." In so doing "it exercises our imaginations" and offers "the lessons of experience, without its tears" (Burney, 1814, p. 7). In short, for Burney, the novelist must clear the weeds of the improbable without sacrificing the imaginative ability to portray a useful if fictional account of the social world, one empirically grounded enough to compel a sense of credibility.

Underwriting the social systems illustrated in *Evelina*, as well as the epistolary mechanism for comparative analysis of the credibility of accounts, is Burney's position that the novel should convey useful precepts through probable renderings of character and circumstance. Gina Campbell has argued that *Evelina* "resembles conduct literature in its emphasis on propriety and that is meant to serve Burney's literary ambitions by teaching her critics how they *ought* to read her work" (Campbell, 1990, p. 557). I argue similarly that this very feature – the conduct-literature approach to enacting Burney's probabilistic theory of the novel – teaches not only critics how to read her, but readers how to make sound judgments in social scenarios. Campbell makes an important observation about the function of epistolary form in *Evelina*, noting "the epistolary novel does not offer" the ability to "establish the nature of a character's motives" because "consciousness of an audience is built into the form," thus, as evinced by the Pamela / anti-Pamela controversy, "a character's repeated reference to her own virtue does not in itself convince us of that virtue" (Campbell, 1990, p. 560). However, the social system or web of relations Burney establishes in the various letters *Evelina* comprises is what supplies the ability to determine character motives along with the credibility of accounts. Campbell observes that "Burney emphasizes the need for a focus on intentionality and interiority by presenting each setback in Evelina's romance [with Lord Orville] twice: once in a social context, where public behavior is the focus of attention, and again in a private context, where motives may be explained" (Campbell, 1990, p. 561).

Burney's novel does not entirely rely on trust in the first-person account. When I suggest it portrays in its letters a social web of testimony, and that this system invites readers to make inferences about credibility of testimony, I mean that we have the opportunity to judge Evelina's descriptions against those of others. The greater benefit of this feature of *Evelina* is that, as we see in Lord Orville's ability to form correct impressions of Evelina's character despite other characters' efforts to mislead him in that regard, Burney's novel foregrounds social judgment in the absence of perfect information by inviting readers to weigh the credibility of written testimony.

The opera Evelina attends ends with a harrowing abduction scene, in which Sir Clement "immediately handed" Evelina into his chariot without her consent and sped off with her, forcing her to call out to the driver and demand he let her off near her lodging, at which point Miss Mervan and Lord Orville witness her leaving the company of Sir Clement. Again Evelina's letter suggests a degree of self-awareness and self-deprecation that lends credence to her account: "My own folly and pride, which had put me in [Sir Clement's] power, were pleas which I could not but attend to in his favour. However, I shall take very particular care never to be again alone with him" (Burney, 1778, p. 101). Putting aside that Evelina is effectively blaming herself for having been forcibly abducted, her intimations to Villars in the letter can do nothing for her concerns about what the scene must have looked like to Orville. "All my joy [at being free of Sir Clement] vanished, and gave place to shame and confusion; for I could not endure that [Orville] should know how long a time Sir Clement and I had been together, since I was not at liberty to assign any reason for it" (Burney, 1778, pp. 98–101).

The degree to which we can say Evelina's assessment of the situation is trustworthy is partly dependent on the degree to which she is convincing to others. Though Rev. Villars only receives her account of the abduction, he finds it all plausible enough believe Sir Clement to be "far more dangerous, because more artful," and Orville to be "a man of sense of of feeling." Villars cautions Evelina specifically against "public and dissipated life" in London, as opposed o the "goodness, honesty, and virtue" of London's "private families," which in turn cautions readers against prejudice or hasty generalization. From this it is possible to build a sense of Villars's credibility and capacity for judgment in tandem with those of Evelina. But again this is something of a self-sealing model of judgment, because Evelina gives an account of her own experiences, and that account in Evelina's letter is Villars's only evidence from which to draw conclusions.

Not until we get to the respectable Lady Howard's letter to Villars, however, can we begin to triangulate our judgment of the impressions given to this point about what Evelina has been through at the opera and at the hands of the conniving Sir Clement. Since Evelina is not part of this correspondence, but the subject of it, we gain access to Lady Howard's corroboration of Evelina's unfavorable judgment of the Branghtons and Madame Duval, as well as details of Duval's scheme to deprive Evelina of her rightful family name and inheritance by way of a lawsuit. Villars disapproves of the lawsuit. Lady Howard also affirms to Villars, who raised Evelina, that "the peculiar attention you have given to her education, has formed her mind to a degree of excellence, that, in one so young, I have scarce ever seen equalled" (Burney, 1778, p. 125). Lady Howard gives us reason to think Evelina's perspective is worth taking seriously, while characters portrayed as foolish, affected, and motivated by frivolity – Madame Duvall and the Branghtons's – perspectives are not. Third-party endorsements (and repudiations) of this sort accomplish what Campbell worries the epistolary form lacks, particularly in Evelina's letters: corroboration of character, judgment, and credibility beyond the first-person account.

This kind of corroboration becomes yet more central to how the plot of *Evelina* unfolds since it eventually falls both to Evelina and to Orville to hold or revise their impressions of one another in the face of an egregious act of deception that threatens to give both of the wrong impression. I refer here to the pivotal moment in the novel at which Evelina decides to pen a letter to Orville, knowing the letter would be received as a social impropriety, to explain that Madame Duvall has stolen Orville's coach in Evelina's name. Duvall, with

Figure 6 Vauxhall Gardens, 1751 (Wales, 1751)

Branghtons in tow, demands use of the coach and scolds Orville's footmen, threatening to "write Lord Orville with word of their ill behaviour without delay." When the footmen ask Duvall which name they should give to Orville to identify who supposedly is entitled to its use, Duvall says "tell him

Miss [Evelina] Anville wants the coach; the young lady he danced with once" (Burney, 1778, p. 246). Duvall's addendum – "the young lady he danced with once" – calls attention to the flimsiness of the social connection she attempts to leverage to gain command of Orville's coach at the expense of Evelina's reputation.

The letter Evelina receives in reply, in Orville's name, turns out to be a forgery by Sir Clement. Copying it as evidence in her letter to Miss Mirvan, and believing it to be from Orville, Evelina writes, "This note, – but let it *speak for itself* [emphasis mine]." The note is sexually forward, opening with "With transport, most charming of thy sex, did I read the letter with which you yesterday morning favoured me," and proposes a clandestine, in-person meeting, as if understanding Evelina's initial letter of apology for and explanation of the coach debacle as a veiled solicitation for a socially inappropriate sexual liaison (Burney, 1778, p. 257). At first Evelina is thrilled that Orville appears to love her, but "upon a second reading, [Evelina] thought every word changed – it did not seem the same letter, – I could not find one sentence that I could look at without blushing: my astonishment was extreme, and it was succeeded by the utmost indignation" (Burney, 1778, p. 258). Indignant and disappointed, Evelina nevertheless models circumspection in this moment. Her exclamation to Miss Mirvan – "I cannot but lament to find myself in a world so deceitful, where we must suspect what we see, distrust what we hear, and doubt even what we feel!" – might seem at first pass an expression of naïveté, though it is also an expression of caution about the strangeness of what she has just read, the fact that it would not seem to comport with what she knows of Orville's character (Burney, 1778, p. 259). By this point in the novel, Burney's readers had had the opportunity to judge accounts of character as well, and undoubtedly find – as Evelina eventually does as well – that something is not quite right with the letter in Orville's name.

Because of Sir Clement's interception and forgery, Orville is in the dark about Evelina's explanation of the coach debacle, while Evelina entertains the belief Orville has been uncharacteristically and thus surprisingly inappropriate with her. When it is eventually revealed that Orville never received her letter of apology, then suspected and later confirmed that Sir Clement was the author of the inappropriate letter to Evelina in Orville's name, both Evelina and Orville also receive confirmation of their initial or intuitive senses that the other is of good character and capable of giving trustworthy accounts. Well before we receive these confirmations, however, Burney has demonstrated the grounds for such appraisals, having built a credibility economy in the novel through the web of impressions and accounts. In contrast to the demonstrated untrustworthiness

of Sir Clement, Madame Duvall, and the Branghtons, Villars, for example, is
hyper-cautious:

> I mean not to depreciate the merit of Lord Orville, who, one mysterious
> instance alone excepted, seems to have deserved the idea you formed of his
> character; but it was not time, it was not knowledge of his worth, obtained
> your regard; your new comrade had not patience to wait any trial; her glowing
> pencil, dipt in the vivid colours of her creative ideas, painted to you, at the
> moment of your first acquaintance, all the excellencies, all the good and rare
> qualities, which a great length of time, and intimacy, could alone have really
> discovered (Burney, 1778, p. 308).

Here Villars, notwithstanding his own protective, conservative instincts, indicates that he finds the Orville letter anomalous on balance, even if he also wishes
Evelina had formed her perspective based on extended experience rather than
testimony. "Dipt in the vivid colours of her creative ideas" recapitulates the
cautious approach to romantic imaginative excess in Burney's preface, while at
the same time reflecting Villars's cautious weighing of evidence. Only "one
mysterious instance alone" marks Orville as suspect in Villars's judgment, but
that is compounded by Villars's impression that Evelina's "heart ... fell the
sacrifice of [her] error," and "was gone ere [she] suspected it was in danger"
(Burney, 1778, p. 308). Yet just as Evelina places significant trust in Villars, she
also lends credence to her experiences with Orville once they resume their
friendship (which eventually becomes their marriage), as when Orville forth-
rightly tells her that when it comes to judgments of propriety, "surely
Miss Anville must be judge for herself! surely she cannot leave the arbitration
of a point so delicate, to one who is ignorant of all the circumstances which
attend it?" (Burney, 1778, p. 299).

As we observe how these characters operate and invest in the credibility
economy Burney constructs, we become implicated in this economy, capable of
forming character judgments from a bird's-eye view of various accounts and
deceptions. I have called this Burney's credibility system or credibility economy because the letters in *Evelina* form a complex network of observations and
judgments that function at one level to pass information between characters and
at another level to model for readers who is and isn't trustworthy and on what
bases. That is, to show how errors, deceptions, and competing accounts and
impressions do not simply self-synthesize; rather, we need to make judgments
about their relative merits and make inferences from the evidence they furnish.
Though it may seem counterintuitive, this aspect of social epistemology – the
networked nature of knowledge and the sociality of the process by which ideas
and judgments become credible – is at the heart of eighteenth-century novels
that imagine and depict the stakes for young women in Evelina's circumstances.

The state of naïveté or of not knowing is inevitable for any neophyte; the social judgments required to know better were of grave importance.

Of course, any epistolary novel in the period could offer something of the perspectival testing or triangulation of accounts as a means of judging credibility; that much is part of the form. But in offering a young, female character in Evelina, what Burney does in particular is put pressure on the importance of credibility for further social judgments. If one kind of anti-Pamela novel was the parody of how incredible Pamela appeared to readers such as Fielding and Haywood, we might understand *Evelina* as another kind, which takes seriously the idea that a woman – whether character or author – would be under considerable pressure to demonstrate credibility as well as to judge it. In this way Burney's contribution to social epistemology in the eighteenth century exceeds that of Richardson as an early writer of novels of testimony.

Conclusion

In *Shame and Necessity*, the philosopher Bernard Williams addresses a question about thought experiments in philosophy: Instead of taking examples from literature, "why not take examples from life?" He answers with a quip that both supports and complicates what I have ventured to accomplish in this Element. "What philosophers will lay before themselves and their readers as an alternative to literature," writes Williams, "will not be life, but bad literature." For Williams, "even when philosophy is not involved in history, it has to make demands on literature." The reason I say Williams's outlook lends support to my argument that eighteenth-century British novels make important contributions to empirical knowledge is that Williams has been very deliberate, in *Shame and Necessity* and in other work, about reserving a place for literature in the pursuit of knowledge, in "seeking a reflective understanding of ethical life," and even in helping us get closer to the truth of things (Williams, 2008, p. 13). Yet when Williams claims that philosophical thought experiments drawn from life rather than literature would be "bad literature," he raises an important question for those interested in the eighteenth-century British novel, particularly its contributions to philosophy. If realism is a fictional, verisimilar preoccupation with life as it is, does that mean realist fiction is a kind of "bad literature," and in turn less useful to philosophy than some of us would like to think?

Scholars of eighteenth-century novels will be familiar with the judgment that our objects of study are "bad" (ask someone to name their favorite novel – even their favorite "realist" novel – and chances are they won't pick from the likes of *Robinson Crusoe, The Female Quixote,* or *Evelina*). As I suggested in the introduction, this is partly due to the fact that the professional study of literature in the Anglophone world arose well after the eighteenth-century novel and organized itself around the study of post-eighteenth-century notions of literature (Literature), culture (Culture), and "literary" aesthetics. Against this backdrop, the eighteenth-century British novel can appear staid, disorganized, slapstick, over-literal, moralizing, and frustratingly discursive. However, this gap between eighteenth-century novels and the aesthetic sensibilities we've come to associate with "good" or "classic" literature is not quite what Williams meant by "bad literature." Williams continues:

> In contrasting philosophy and literature, we should remember that some philosophy is itself literature. Philosophers often suppose that the kinds of difficulties raised for them by a literary text are not presented by texts they classify as philosophical, but this idea is produced largely by the selective way in which they use them. We should bear in mind how drastically some of these texts are being treated when they are read in this way. The kind of treatment that is needed in order to extract from the text what philosophers mostly look for, argumentative structures, obviously demands more restructuring of some texts than others, and the texts that need the most drastic regimentation may sometimes yield the most interesting results. But this does not mean that those texts do not present literary problems of how they should be read; indeed they present such problems to people trying to decide how to regiment them. (Williams, 2008, p. 13)

The epistemic value of the novels of Defoe, Lennox, and Burney, among others, comes not simply from their engagement with the formula of the problem of correspondence plus the problem of representation, but from the various ways these novels discuss and model conceptual problems (such as the reliability of sense perception) and methods of establishing knowledge (such as social or collective reasoning about judgments of credibility). And when such models and methods in the eighteenth-century novel demand that authors and readers take interest in the particulars of everyday life, the novel dwells not only on verisimilar or probabilistic representations but also on methods and processes of inference. When Williams makes the incisive point that even texts we approach as works of philosophy can pose literary problems, and therefore that extracting useful argumentative structures from texts frequently requires some "restructuring" and "regimentation," he implies a corollary point about literature. Like philosophical work that makes demands on literature and literary analysis, literature itself can contain models and argumentative structures of philosophical value.

On this point, consider Williams's explanation, in *Truth and Truthfulness*, of the value of fiction as a model for pursuing truth. Taking up the example of

Robert Nozick's explanation of the "State of Nature," Williams notes that Nozick starts with the idea of "potential explanation," or in Nozick's words an explanation that "would be the correct explanation if everything in it were true and operated." For Williams, therefore, a "*law-defective* potential explanation is a potential explanation with a false law-like statement, while a *fact-defective* potential explanation has a false antecedent condition. Some explanations that are fact-defective but not law-defective are useful because they show that a process is *possible*" (Williams, 2002, p. 31). In the pursuit of truth, per Williams, "there is … a role for a fictional narrative, an imagined developmental story, which helps to explain a concept or value or institution by showing ways in which it could have come about in a simplified environment containing certain kinds of human interests or capacities, which, relative to the story, are taken as given" (Williams, 2002, p. 21).

A few things here are crucial to observe. One, the philosophical language of law-defective versus fact-defective potential explanations is another way of conceptualizing the capacity of novels to model processes of knowledge production, and in so doing to illustrate how one might work through epistemic problems. In the context of the eighteenth-century British novel, fact-defectiveness is a function of the inability of any strategy of representation, no matter how "realist," to transmit knowledge unto itself. Novels are fact-defective by virtue of having false antecedent conditions (fictionality), but are not necessarily law-defective. Their illustrations of rationale and methods of inference bring readers through the challenges of epistemic problems in ways that are both analogous to and useful for inferring from data in life as in fiction. Two, Williams's language – "taken as given" – recapitulates the epistemological function of the novel of data, novelistic data as a basis for thought experiment. We can take novelistic data as "given" in the axiomatic sense – as opposed to the quixotic sense, as *real* – as a basis from which to reason through the thought experiments it occasions. Three, Williams's language – "ways in which it could have come about" – is indicative of the world of the possible as well as the probable, which is the basis of novelistic or "realist" strategies of representation. Four, the "simplified environment containing certain kinds of human interests or capacities" is akin to the worlds created by eighteenth-century novelists. Consider, for example, Crusoe's account of scavenging in the shipwreck to find the supplies he needs to survive as a basis for showing *how one might survive under such conditions*. Literature scholars understandably privilege the aesthetics of textual complexity and the work of pointing it out, but fictionalizing is not always or necessarily an act of complexification. Like experimentation, it's often an act of reduction, as when spare prose serves certain aesthetic objectives, or, as I've shown, contriving certain social and epistemic scenarios serves thought experiment. When readers observe the wildly improbable in the endings of so many eighteenth-century British novels, we're observing a form of useful reduction, not – as many critics would have it – a form of aesthetic failure.

As we've seen in *The Female Quixote*, Lennox brings quixotism to bear on the problem of perception, not just by couching in fiction a series of arguments about problems of sense perception, but also by imagining scenarios in which the assumptions of empirical knowledge as perceptual knowledge might reach their breaking points. In *Evelina*, Burney offers a social model of judging the credibility of testimony, an essential concept for the establishment of knowledge. From each of these novels readers can extract what Williams calls argumentative structures, perhaps most clearly in the case of Arabella's conversation with the doctor toward the conclusion of *The Female Quixote*. But novels can also do epistemology by modeling concepts, networks, and thought experiments in the manner that Williams describes in his arguments about the value of fiction in philosophical projects.

The study of knowledge in the eighteenth-century novel – or the epistemology of the novel – is not only valuable for philosophy; it also has the capacity to fundamentally change how scholars of literature have long understood the concept of novelistic realism. From the beginning, following Ian Watt's diagnosis of the eighteenth-century novel's "formal realism," even scholars that have revised Watt's account have taken realism as both a *formal* feature, or something that might constitutively mark the novel as a genre, and an effort to offer, in Watt's words, "a full and authentic report of human experience" (Watt, 2001, p. 32). Viewed as a form and as a report, novelistic realism has struggled under the weight of scholarly reassessment. Peter Boxall, for example, argues that "realism has fallen today into a kind of suspension or quite radical uncertainty," because "one of the shared assumptions that make realism possible . . . reveals itself to have been based all along on a false premise." This Boxall concludes based on a reading of J. M. Coetzee's *Elizabeth Costello* (2003). In Coetzee's novel, Costello gives a talk entitled "What Is Realism?," based on her reading of Franz Kafka's "A Report to the Academy," a story of an ape called Red Peter who learns human language and behavior and explains this process to a group of academics. As Boxall explains, for Costello, the formal properties of Kafka's text "allow us no purchase on its truth value, no capacity to gauge the nature of its realism." The false premise, in other words, is that there's some kind of formal property particular to the novel that grants us purchase on the real, a formal strategy of representation that exceeds the fidelity of representation in other genres (Boxall, 2015, pp. 40–41).

In my view – following from the arguments I've made in this Element – both the proponents and the skeptics of novelistic realism are missing the point. That is, for proponents, conceiving of realism in terms of the problem of correspondence plus the problem of representation misses Williams's observation that what differentiates the texts we call literature and the texts we call philosophy is often our approaches to these, rather than some constitutive formal property or properties of the texts themselves. In other words, the effort to define the novel in formal terms as a distinct genre with a distinct formal signature – rather than as an instance in the history of writing that reflects multiple generic conventions and motivations drawn together in a time and place of epistemic rupture – has always risked aestheticizing the novel's contribution to knowledge in untenable ways. For skeptics of novelistic realism, focusing on the very fact that formal realism is an untenable proposition has bolstered an anti-cognitivist view of the novel from another direction: not aestheticizing the novel's contributions to knowledge, but denying the very premise that the novel makes contributions to knowledge at all, at least by any way other than as a failed realist experiment. I hope that in the foregoing sections I've given readers enough to question not only this view but the broader view that formal realism is the best framework for understanding the novel's contribution to knowledge. The primary epistemic innovation of the eighteenth-century novel was not representation, but method.

References

Alkon, P. (1979). *Defoe and Fictional Time*, Athens: University of Georgia Press.

Arbuthnot, J. (1701). *An Essay on the Usefulness of Mathematical Learning*, Oxford: Printed at the Theatre in Oxford for Anth. Priestley.

Auyoung, E. (2020). What We Mean by Reading. *New Literary History* 51(1), 93–114.

Bacon, F. (1620). *The Philosophical Works of Frances Bacon*, Repr 1905, London: Routledge.

Bannet, E. T. (2007). Quixotes, Imitations, and Transatlantic Genres. *Eighteenth-Century Studies* 40(4), 553–569.

Batten, W. (1630). *A Most Plaine and Easie Way for Finding the Sunne's Amplitude and Azimuth*, London.

Bender, J. (1998). Enlightenment Fiction and the Scientific Hypothesis. *Representations* 61(Winter), 6–28.

Bender, J. (2010). Novel Knowledge: Judgment, Experience, Experiment, in Siskin, C. and Warner, W. (eds.) *This Is Enlightenment*, Chicago: University of Chicago Press, pp. 284–300.

Bender, J. (2012). *Ends of Enlightenment*, Stanford: Stanford University Press.

Berkeley, G. (1710). *Principles of Human Knowledge and Three Dialogues*, Repr 2009, Oxford: Oxford University Press.

Bowker, G. and Star, S. L. (1999). *Sorting Things Out: Classification and its Consequences*, Cambridge, MA: MIT Press.

Boxall, P. (2015). *The Value of the Novel*, Cambridge: Cambridge University Press.

Boyle, R. (1661). *Robert Boyle's Air-Pump*. Accessed August 5, 2022. https://commons.wikimedia.org/wiki/File:Boyle_air_pump.jpg.

Burney, F. (1778). *Evelina*, Repr 2008, Oxford: Oxford University Press.

Burney, F. (1814). *The Wanderer*, Repr 2001, Oxford: Oxford University Press.

Campbell, G. (1990). How to Read Like a Gentleman: Burney's Instructions to Her Critics in *Evelina*. *English Literary History* 57(3), 557–583.

Campbell, M. B. (1999). *Wonder and Science: Imagining Worlds in Early Modern Europe*, Ithaca: Cornell University Press.

Cheyne, G. (1701). *A New Theory of Continu'd Fevers*, Edinburgh.

Chico, T. (2018). *The Experimental Imagination: Literary Knowledge and Science in the British Enlightenment*, Stanford: Stanford University Press.

Crump, J. (2002). *A Known Scribbler: Frances Burney on Literary Life*, Peterborough: Broadview.

Dale, A. (2019). *The Printed Reader: Gender, Quixotism, and Textual Bodies in Eighteenth-Century Britain*, Lewisburg: Bucknell University Press.

Daston, L. and Galison, P. (2007). *Objectivity*, New York: Zone Books.

Defoe, D. (1719). *Robinson Crusoe*, Repr 2007, Oxford: Oxford University Press.

DeGabriele, P. (2014). The Legal Fiction and Epistolary Form: Frances Burney's *Evelina*. *Journal for Early Modern Cultural Studies* 14(2), 22–40.

Deringer, W. (2018). *Calculated Values: Finance, Politics, and the Quantitative Age*, Cambridge, MA: Harvard University Press.

Dicker, G. (2019). *Locke on Knowledge and Reality: A Commentary on an Essay Concerning Human Understanding*, Oxford: Oxford University Press.

Donnelly, B. (2019). "Chequer Works of Providence": Skeptical Providentialism in Daniel Defoe's Fiction. *Philosophy and Literature* 43, 107–120.

Doody, M. A. (1997). The Short Fiction, in Copeland, E. and McMaster, J. (eds.) *The Cambridge Companion to Jane Austen*, Cambridge: Cambridge University Press, pp. 84–99.

Doré, G. (1863). *Don Quijote and Sancho Panza*. Accessed August 5, 2022. https://commons.wikimedia.org/wiki/File:Don_Quijote_and_Sancho_Panza .jpg.

Evelyn, J. (1667). *Frontispiece to the History of the Royal Society of London*. 1702 ed. Accessed August 5, 2022. https://commons.wikimedia.org/wiki/File:Frontispiece_to_%27The_History_of_the_Royal-Society_of_London %27.jpg.

Fielding, H. (1741). *Shamela*, Repr 2008, Oxford: Oxford University Press.

Fielding, H. (1742). *Joseph Andrews*, Repr 2008, Oxford: Oxford University Press.

Fielding, H. (1749). *Tom Jones*, Repr 1998, Oxford: Oxford University Press.

Fielding, H. (1752). Review of Charlotte Lennox's *The Female Quixote*. *The Covent Garden Journal* 242, Repr 2011.

Gallagher, C. (2006). The Rise of Fictionality, in Moretti, F. (ed.) *The Novel*, Princeton: Princeton University Press, pp. 336–363.

Gordon, S. P. (2006). *The Practice of Quixotism: Postmodern Theory and Eighteenth-Century Women's Writing*, New York: Palgrave.

Grayling, A. C. (2019). *The History of Philosophy*, New York: Penguin.

Hacking, I. (1975). *The Emergence of Probability: A Philosophical Study of Early Ideas about Probability, Induction, and Statistical Inference*, Repr 2006, Cambridge: Cambridge University Press.

Hanlon, A. R. (2019). *A World of Disorderly Notions: Quixote and the Logic of Exceptionalism*, Charlottesville: University of Virginia Press.

Hanlon, A. R. (forthcoming a). From Writing Lives to Scaling Lives in Joseph Priestley's *Chart of Biography*. *The Eighteenth Century: Theory and Interpretation* 62(3–4).

Hanlon, A. R. (forthcoming b). Information and Credibility in *Journal of the Plague Year*. *Digital Defoe*.

Hanlon, A. R. (forthcoming c). *Sense and Sensibility* as Social-Epistemic System. *Studies in the Novel* 55(2).

Hastings, W. (1912). Errors and Inconsistencies in Defoe's *Robinson Crusoe*. *English Language Notes* 27(6), pp. 161–166.

Hershinow, S. (2019). *Born Yesterday: Inexperience and the Early Realist Novel*, Baltimore: Johns Hopkins University Press.

Hooke, R. (1665a). *Micrographia*, London: printed by Jo. Martyn and Ja. Allestry, printers to the Royal Society.

Hooke, R. (1665b). *Stinging Nettle*. Accessed August 5, 2022. https://commons .wikimedia.org/wiki/File:Robert_Hooke,_Micrographia,_stinging_nettle._ Wellcome_L0013027.jpg.

Hume, D. (1739). *A Treatise of Human Nature*, Repr 2000, Oxford: Oxford University Press.

Hume, D. (1748). *An Enquiry Concerning Human Understanding*, Repr 2008, Oxford: Oxford University Press.

Hume, D. (1757). *Of the Standard of Taste, and Other Essays*, Repr 1965, Indianapolis: Bobbs-Merrill.

Keiser, J. (2020). *Nervous Fictions: Literary Form and the Enlightenment Origins of Neuroscience*, Charlottesville: University of Virginia Press.

Kirkley, H. (2002). *A Biographer at Work: Samuel Johnson's Notes for the "Life of Pope"*, Lewisburg: Bucknell University Press.

Kramnick, J. (2007). Empiricism, Cognitive Science, and the Novel. *The Eighteenth Century: Theory and Interpretation* 48(3), 263–285.

Kramnick, J. (2010). *Actions and Objects from Hobbes to Richardson*, Stanford: Stanford University Press.

Kukkonen, K. (2019). *4E Cognition and Eighteenth-Century Fiction: How the Novel Found its Feet*, Oxford: Oxford University Press.

Lake, C. (2020). *Artifacts: How We Think and Write about Found Objects*, Baltimore: Johns Hopkins University Press.

Lakoff, G. and Johnson, M. (1999). *Philosophy in the Flesh: The Embodied Mind and its Challenge to Western Thought*, New York: Basic Books.

Lamb, J. (2007). Locke's Wild Fancies: Empiricism, Personhood, and Fictionality. *The Eighteenth Century: Theory and Interpretation* 48(3), 187–204.

Lennox, C. (1752). *The Female Quixote*, Repr 2008, Oxford: Oxford University Press.

Loar, C. (2019). Plague's Ecologies: Daniel Defoe and the Epidemic Constitution. *Eighteenth-Century Fiction* 32(1), 31–53.

Longino, H. (1990). *Science as Social Knowledge: Values and Objectivity in Scientific Inquiry*, Princeton: Princeton University Press.

Lupton, C. (2012). *Knowing Books: The Consciousness of Mediation in Eighteenth-Century Britain*, Philadelphia: University of Pennsylvania Press.

MacDonnell, K. (2020). Beneath Defoe's Island: Imperial Geopolitics and the Inorganic Economy in *Robinson Crusoe*. *Philological Quarterly* 99(1), 1–24.

Maioli, R. (2016). *Empiricism and the Early Theory of the Novel*, London: Palgrave.

McKeon, M. (2000). *Theory of the Novel: A Historical Approach*, Baltimore: Johns Hopkins University Press.

Molesworth, J. (2010). *Chance and the Eighteenth-Century Novel: Realism, Probability, Magic*, Cambridge: Cambridge University Press.

Motooka, W. (1998). *The Age of Reasons: Quixotism, Sentimentalism, and Political Economy in Eighteenth-Century Britain*, London: Routledge.

Okasha, S. (2001). What Did Hume Really Show about Induction? *The Philosophical Quarterly* 51(204), 307–327.

Oldenburg, H. (1666). *Philosophical Transactons Volume 1 Frontispiece*. Accessed August 5, 2022. https://commons.wikimedia.org/wiki/File: Philosophical_Transactions_Volume_1_frontispiece.jpg.

Oreskes, N. (2019). *Why Trust Science?* Princeton: Princeton University Press.

Paulson, R. (1998). *Don Quixote in England: The Aesthetics of Laughter*, Baltimore: Johns Hopkins University Press.

Petty, W. (1690). *Political Arithmetick*, London: Printed for *Robert Clavel* at the *Peacock*, and *Hen. Mortlock* at the *Phoenix* in St. *Paul's* Church-yard.

Picciotto, J. (2010). *Labors of Innocence in Early Modern England*, Cambridge, MA: Harvard University Press.

Pino, M. (2010). Burney's *Evelina* and Aesthetics in Action. *Modern Philology* 108(2), 263–303.

Poovey, M. (1998). *A History of the Modern Fact: Problems of Knowledge in the Sciences of Wealth and Society*, Chicago: University of Chicago Press.

Porter, T. (1995). *Trust in Numbers: The Pursuit of Objectivity in Science and Public Life*, Princeton: Princeton University Press.

Porter, D. (2018). *Science, Form, and the Problem of Induction*, Cambridge: Cambridge University Press.

Preston, C. (2016). *The Poetics of Scientific Investigation in Seventeenth-Century England*, Oxford: Oxford University Press.

Priest, S. (2007). *The British Empiricists*, London: Routledge.

Principe, L. M. (1995). Virtuous Romance and Romantic Virtuoso: The Shaping of Robert Boyle's Literary Style. *Journal of the History of Ideas* 56(3), 377–397.

Rickless, S. (2008). Is Locke's Theory of Knowledge Inconsistent? *Philosophy and Phenomenological Research* 77(1), 83–104.

Rosenberg, D. (2013). Data before the Fact, in Gitelman, L. (ed.) *Raw Data is an Oxymoron*, Cambridge, MA: MIT Press, pp. 15–40.

Schaffer, S. (2020). *We are Interested in What Happens When People Disagree*. Accessed August 18, 2020. www.uab.cat/web?cid=1096481466574&pagename=UABDivulga%2FPage%2FTemplatePageDetallArticleInvestigar&param1=1321342540533.

Schmidgen, W. (2001). Robinson Crusoe, Enumeration, and the Mercantile Fetish. *Eighteenth-Century Studies* 35(1), 19–39.

Schmidgen, W. (2016). The Metaphysics of *Robinson Crusoe*. *English Literary History* 83(1), 101–126.

Shapin, S. (1995). Cordelia's Love: Credibility and the Social Study of Science. *Perspectives on Science* 3(3), 255–275.

Shapin, S. and Schaffer, S. (2011). *Leviathan and the Air-Pump: Hobbes, Boyle, and the Experimental Life*, revised ed., Princeton: Princeton University Press.

Siskin, C. (2001). Novels and Systems. *NOVEL: A Forum on Fiction* 34(2), 202–215.

Smith, C. W. (2016). *Empiricist Devotions: Science, Religion, and Poetry in Early Eighteenth-Century England*, Charlottesville: University of Virginia Press.

Spacks, P. M. (1974). Ev'ry Woman is at Heart a Rake. *Eighteenth-Century Studies* 8(1), 27–46.

Spacks, P. M. (1988). The Subtle Sophistry of Desire: Dr. Johnson and *The Female Quixote*. *Modern Philology* 85, 532–542.

Spacks, P. M. (1990). *Desire and Truth: Functions of Plot in Eighteenth-Century English Novels*, Chicago: University of Chicago Press.

Straub, K. (1989). Reconstructing the Gaze: Voyeurism in Richardson's *Pamela*. *Studies in Eighteenth-Century Culture* 18, 419–431.

Swenson, R. (2010). Optics, Gender, and the Eighteenth-Century Gaze: Looking at Eliza Haywood's *Anti-Pamela*. *The Eighteenth Century: Theory and Interpretation* 51(1–2), 27–43.

Thompson, H. (2016). *Fictional Matter: Empiricism, Corpuscles, and the Novel*, Philadelphia: University of Pennsylvania Press.

Thompson, H. and Meeker, N. (2007). Empiricism, Substance, Narrative: An Introduction. *The Eighteenth Century: Theory and Interpretation* 48(3), 183–186.

Vickers, B. (2002). "Words" and "Things" – or, "Words, Concepts, and Things"? Rhetorical and Linguistic Categories in the Renaissance, in Kessler, E. and Maclean, I. (eds.) *Res et Verba in der Renaissance*, Weissbaden: Harassowitz Verglag, pp. 287–335.

Wales, S. (1751). *A Prospect of Vauxhall Gardens*. Accessed August 5, 2022. https://commons.wikimedia.org/wiki/File:Vauxhall_Gardens_by_ Samuel_Wale_c1751.jpg.

Warner, W. (1998). *Licensing Entertainment: The Elevation of Novel Reading in Britain, 1684–1750*, Berkeley: University of California Press.

Watt, I. (1957). *The Rise of the Novel*, Berkeley: University of California Press.

Watt, I. (2001). *The Rise of the Novel: Studies in Defoe, Richardson, and Fielding*, 2nd ed., Berkeley: University of California Press.

Williams, B. (2002). *Truth and Truthfulness: An Essay in Genealogy*, Princeton: Princeton University Press.

Williams, B. (2008). *Shame and Necessity*, 2nd ed., Berkeley: University of California Press.

Wong, B. (2016). *Pamela, Part II*: Richardson's Trial by Theatre. *Eighteenth-Century Fiction* 29(2), 179–199.

Wood, J. (2020). Robinson Crusoe and the Earthly Ground. *Eighteenth-Century Fiction* 32(3), 381–406.

Wood, S. (2005). *Quixotic Fictions of the USA, 1792–1815*, Oxford: Oxford University Press.

Wragge-Morley, A. (2020). *Aesthetic Science: Representing Nature in the Royal Society of London, 1650–1720*, Chicago: University of Chicago Press.

Cambridge Elements ≡

Eighteenth-Century Connections

Printed in the United States
by Baker & Taylor Publisher Services